AFRICAN PERSPECTIVES ON COLONIALISM

A. Adu Boahen

THE JOHNS HOPKINS UNIVERSITY PRESS   BALTIMORE, MARYLAND

© 1987 The Johns Hopkins University Press
All rights reserved. Published 1987
Printed in the United States of America on acid-free paper

The Johns Hopkins University Press
2715 North Charles Street, Baltimore, Maryland 21218-4363
www.press.jhu.edu

Johns Hopkins Paperbacks edition, 1989
9

LIBRARY OF CONGRESS CATALOGING-IN-PUBLICATION DATA
Boahen, A. Adu.
African perspectives on colonialism
(The Johns Hopkins symposia in comparative history; 15th)
"1985 James S. Schouler lectures" – Pref.
Bibliography: p 121
Includes index.
1. Colonies – Africa – History. 2. Africa – Colonial influence – History.
I. Title II. Series
JV246.B63 1987 325.6 87-2769
ISBN 0-8018-3456-2
ISBN 0-8018-3931-9 (pbk)

A catalog record for this book is available from the British Library.

Contents

Preface

I t was not easy to choose a theme for the James S. Schouler lecture series, and it was only after long reflection and analysis that I decided on the present topic. There are two main reasons for my choice. First, although there is no theme in African history on which more has been written than that of the rise and fall of colonialism in Africa,[1] most of these authors have looked at the subject primarily from an Euro-centric point of view. Their principal preoccupations, in spite of the recent noise that has been made about African resistance, have been the origins, structure, operation, and impact of colonialism. The crucial questions of how *Africans* perceived colonialism, what initiatives and responses they displayed in the face of this colonial challenge, and above all how they reacted after the forcible imposition of colonialism have not been systematically dealt with. I am not saying that these themes have never been treated elsewhere. They have been, indeed, ever since the epoch-making international conference at the University of Dar es Salaam in October 1965. My purpose here is to attempt a synthesis of all these materials scattered in various learned journals, anthologies, and books, and especially in the recently published volume 7 of the UNESCO *General History of Africa*, of which I am the editor.[2]

Secondly, 1985 marked the twenty-fifth anniversary of the overthrow of colonialism in Africa, and many conferences and seminars were held to assess what independence has meant for Africans, one of them in January 1985 at Harare in Zimbabwe and another in July in Nigeria. I chose this theme, then, to give the necessary historical background to the independence revolution that occurred in the 1960s.

I would like to express my gratitude to the chairman and the members of the Department of History at the Johns Hopkins University for inviting me to give the 1985 James S. Schouler Lectures. I am particularly grateful to Professor John Russell-Wood for his warm friendship, his hospitality, and the efficient way in which he organized the lectures. I also feel highly indebted to Professor Philip Curtin and his wife, Pat, who not only accommodated me in their beautiful home but also did all they could to make my stay there as socially entertaining and academically rewarding as possible; in addition, Professor Curtin took the trouble to go through the lectures and send me useful comments and suggestions. Finally, I should not fail to mention Henry Y. K. Tom, the senior social sciences editor of the Johns Hopkins University Press, whose subtle pressure and carefully worded reminders compelled me to complete the preparation of the lectures for publication. Apart from a few sections that I rewrote, these lectures are published as they were delivered.

AFRICAN PERSPECTIVES ON COLONIALISM

CHAPTER ONE

The Eve of the Colonial Conquest and Occupation

The most surprising aspects of the imposition of colonialism on Africa were its suddenness and its unpredictability. By as late as 1880, there were no real signs or indications of this phenomenal and catastrophic event. On the contrary, an overwhelming majority of the states and polities of Africa were enjoying their sovereign existence, and their rulers were in full control of their own affairs and destinies. Indeed, Africa had experienced a series of far-reaching revolutions during the first eight decades of the nineteenth century and by 1880 was in a mood of optimism and seemed poised for a major breakthrough on all fronts. By 1880, old Africa appeared to be in its dying throes, and a new and modern Africa was emerging. In this opening chapter, I shall analyze these internal dynamics, which were not only economic and political but above all social and intellectual; I shall paint a picture of what Africa was on the eve of the colonial conquest and occupation as a result of these internal dynamics; and I shall analyze the mood of Africans as articulated by their principal spokesmen, namely, their traditional rulers and leaders.

The first and the most important of the economic changes that had occurred in Africa by 1880 was the abolition and suppression of that most inhuman and abominable of all trading activities — namely, the slave trade — and its replacement by trade in natural products, which has become known in typical Eurocentric terms as legitimate trade. At the beginning of the nineteenth century, the external economy of virtually the whole of Africa depended on the slave trade to the Americas, the Indian Ocean islands and India, Europe, and the Middle East. The slave trade across the Indian Ocean from eastern and central Africa in fact reached its peak during the first five decades of the century. By 1880, however, thanks mainly to the anti–slave trade activities of the British naval squadron, the slave trade across the Atlantic had been completely suppressed, the trans-Saharan traffic had dwindled to a mere trickle, and the central and eastern African branch had virtually dried up.

That the abolition and suppression of the slave trade came as a shock to many Africans and posed a great challenge to them cannot be denied. The first reaction is evident from the very interesting and illuminating discussion that took place in 1820 between Joseph Dupuis, the British consul sent to Kumasi, the capital of the Asante empire, and the Asantehene, Osei Bonsu:

"Now," said the king, after a pause, "I have another palaver, and you must help me to talk it. A long time ago the great king liked plenty of trade, more than now; then many ships came, and they brought ivory, gold and slaves; but now he will not let the ships come as before, and the people buy gold and ivory only. This is what I have in my head, so now tell me truly, like a friend, why does the king do so?" "His majesty's question," I replied, "was connected with a great palaver, which my instructions did not authorise me to discuss. I had nothing to say regarding the slave trade. . . ."

Taking up one of my observations, he remarked, "the white men who go to council with your master, and pray to the great God for him, do not understand my country, or they would not say the slave trade was bad. But if they think it bad now, why did they think it good before. Is not your law an old law, the same as the Crammo (Moslem) law? Do you not both serve the same God, only you have different fashions and customs? Crammos are strong people in festishe, and they say the law is good, because the great God made the book; so they buy slaves, and teach them good things, which they knew not before. . . . If the great king would like to restore this trade it would be good for the white men and for me too. . . ."

I urged the impossibility of the king's request, promising, however, to record his sentiments faithfully. "Well then," said the king, "you must put down in my master's book all I shall say, and then he will look to it, now he is my friend. And when he sees what is true, he will surely restore that trade. I cannot make war to catch slaves in the bush, like a thief. My ancestors never did so. But if I fight a king, and kill him when

ATLANTIC OCEAN

CANARY ISLANDS

Tlemcen
Algiers
Sp.
Fr.
ALGIERS
Tu.
Tunis
Fez
Tripoli
Benghazi
Alexandria
Port Said
TRIPOLITANIA
CYRENAICA
Tu.
Cairo
Sijilmasa
FEZZAN
Murzuk
EGYPT
Asyut
Insalah
Taghaza
Ghat

Shinqlt
Fr.
DAKAR
Niger
Timbuctu
Bilma
Bathurst
FULA
Gao
KANEM
KORDOFAN
Br.
KAARTA
MACINA
Agades
L.Chad
Abechi
El Farsher
TUKULOR EMPIRE
GURMA
BORNO
WADAI
MAHDIST STATE
SAMORI'S EMPIRE
MAMPRUSI
DAGOMBA
FULANI EMPIRE
Freetown
Br.
ASANTE
FANTE
YORUBA
Abeokuta
IBO
Addis Ababa
ETHIOPIA
Fr.
Accra
Lagos
Br.
BENIN
Coutonou
Br.
Fr.
Duala
FANG
R.Congo
Kibale
BABUA
BUNYORO
BUGANDA
KIKUYU
Mogadishu
GABON
Fr.
BUDJA
KAMBA
L.Victoria
MASAI

ATLANTIC OCEAN

LUNDA
YAKA
ANKOLE
RUANDA
BURUNDI
L.Tanganyika
ZANZIBAR
Dar es Salaam
BAKONGO
MATAMBA
KASANJE
Mwata
YEKE
SWAHILI
HEHE
Kilwa
L.Nyasa
Luanda
LUBA
NGONI
Po.
LUNDA
KAZEMBE
YAO
Mozambique
Benguela
Po.
KATANGA
R.Zambezi
MARAVI EMPIRE
Po.
Beira
MERINA KINGDOM
Tananarive
LOZI
BUTWA
Belagoa Bay
SWAZI
GAZA
R.Orange
ZULU
ORANGE FREE STATE
CAPE COLONY
GRIQUA
Cape Town
Br.
Port Elizabeth

- - - Trade Routes
Fr.   French
Br.   British
Sp.   Spanish
Po.   Portuguese
Tu.   Turkish

0   500   1000   1500 Km

INDIAN OCEAN

AFRICAN PEOPLES AND STATES ON THE EVE OF PARTITION AND CONQUEST

he is insolent, then certainly I must have his gold, and his slaves, and
the people are mine too. Do not the white kings act like this?"[1]

The British government did not, of course, agree to renew the
slave trade, and both Osei Bonsu and the other African rulers
and merchants had to face the challenge posed by the suppression. It says a lot for their resourcefulness and adaptability that
by 1880 they had succeeded in filling the huge economic vacuum
created by the cessation of the slave trade. By that date, instead
of human beings, the mainstays of Africa's external economy

were ivory, gum or copal, cloves, beeswax, honey, wild coffee, peanuts, cotton, and above all rubber. Indeed, in Ghana, not only had rubber become the second leading export — the first being palm oil — but by 1891 Ghana had become the leading producer of rubber in the British empire and the third in the world. In eastern, central, and equatorial Africa, ivory had become the leading export, followed by wax and copal, and after 1870, rubber. It is reported that by the 1860s "ivory moving down the Congo . . . by way of Stanley Pool amounted to a sixth of all the ivory that was marketed in London, and . . . by the early 1880s the annual value of trade at the mouth of the Congo was about 3 million pounds sterling."[2]

The consequences of this revolutionary change from the slave trade to trade in natural products were truly phenomenal. First, the steady diminution of the slave trade meant a corresponding cessation of the wars and raids that produced the slaves and, with that, the beginning of peace and stability in those regions of the continent that had been the principal sources of that inhuman traffic. Another significant consequence of this change, one often ignored by many historians, was a more equitable distribution of wealth, especially in the rural areas of Africa. Most of the products involved in the new export activity were growing wild and could be collected by all and sundry, especially those living in the rural areas; others, such as ivory, could be obtained through hunting. This meant that unlike the slave trade, which could be indulged in mainly by the ruling aristocracy and a few powerful entrepreneurs with the resources to create and maintain large bands of personal followers or armies, this new trade — obtained from what has been described as a "gathering-based economy" — could be indulged in by everybody, and by those living in the urban as well as in the rural areas. By 1880, therefore, wealth was ceasing to be the exclusive monopoly of the ruling aristocracy and the relatively few mercantile families or clans such as the Dyula (or Juula, meaning "merchant" in Malinke) of the savanna areas of West Africa and the Swahili traders of East Africa and was becoming steadily diffused throughout every society. This development was to gain even greater momentum in the colonial period with the more systematic promotion of the cultivation and production of cash crops such as cocoa and peanuts on peasant and not plantation basis. This interesting development led to the emergence of a nouveau riche, both male and female, in the rural areas; a great increase in the number of entrepreneurs in the former urban and market centers; and the beginnings of rural capitalism. The third consequence of the change was demographic and will be discussed later.

The fourth consequence of the transition from the slave trade to the export of natural products was that by 1880, not only the external or coastal economy but even more importantly the internal or rural economy of Africa had become more deeply integrated into the capitalist world-economy than before, a development which the ensuing colonial system was to intensify. The final and most important consequence was the alteration of the status of the African himself. From being a mere commodity, the African now became a human being in his own right, himself producing commodities for sale. This crucial change in status meant the removal of one of the main constraints in the overall development and progress of Africans.

Besides the changeover from the slave trade to the trade in natural products, the other interesting economic change that had occurred in Africa by 1880 was the completion of the commercial unification of Africa. Although the whole of western and northern Africa had been commercially integrated ever since pre-European times by caravan routes, which grew in complexity with the centuries,[3] there were hardly any routes linking northeastern Africa with central and eastern Africa, nor, more surprisingly, were there any routes running across central Africa even as late as the beginning of the nineteenth century. On the contrary, as Curtin and others have shown, three independent systems of trade had emerged — the Atlantic, the Mediterranean and the Indian Ocean coasts systems.[4] The first covered the present areas of the Republic of Congo, Zaire, and Angola; the second covered the present area of Egypt and the Sudan; and the third, modern Tanzania, Kenya, Malawi, Zambia, and Mozambique.

It was not until the nineteenth century that all these trading systems were linked together both by land and river, especially the Congo and its tributaries. This process began during the first decade of the nineteenth century when two Angolan traders crossed the continent. They were followed by Arab, Swahili, and Nyamwezi traders, who in search of ivory and slaves had pushed their way from the coast of Tanzania beyond Lake Tanganyika by the 1820s; and more and more traders had penetrated even further by the 1850s. In the 1860s the caravans of the Nyamwezi trader Msiri had reached as far west as Katanga and Kazembe, where he had established an empire and from which he dispatched caravans to Benguela on the Atlantic coast and Bagamoyo on the Indian Ocean. The Bisa, Yao, and Chikunde traders of modern Tanzania and Mozambique had also, by the 1850s, entered the Shire Valley and pushed on into contemporary Zimbabwe. By the last three decades of the century, the Ovimbundu, Chokwe, and Tio traders of Angola, similarly in search of ivory, had also pushed their trading activities eastwards across the Kwango River and were transacting business with the Swahili and Nyamwezi traders in the area of the kingdoms of Kazembe and Lunda. It was also during the second half of the century that the Congo and its tributaries were turned into commercial highways which replaced the old overland routes.

In the Nile Valley, traders from Cairo, the Red Sea, and Khartoum also began to extend their trading activities southwards from the Darfur and Kordofan areas and by the 1850s had penetrated as far south as the Bahr-el-Gazal, Azande, and Mangbetu regions, where they met traders from the east and west coasts. Thus, by 1880, all three trade systems had merged in the Azande area, which was to be divided during the Partition among Britain, France, and Belgium.

The linking of these three trading systems through long-distance trade had some far-reaching social and economic consequences. First, the new long-distance networks unified local trade networks, "promoted spatial specialization and helped to give greater elasticity to commercial relations over vast stretches of territory."[5] Secondly, this trade led to the evolution of new social patterns as status acquired through birth gave way to achieved status and a new elite of traders emerged who in some areas, especially in central and equatorial Africa, superseded the old aristocracies. Third, the long-distance trade produced or accelerated the spread of certain lingua francas and cultures. Thus the Swahili culture and language spread from East Africa into the whole of eastern Zaire as well as into the copper areas of modern Zambia. A pidgin language, Lingala, and with it a Lingala culture, evolved and spread in present-day Zaire and the Republic of Congo, while a new Zande-Mangbetu culture evolved in equatorial Africa. By 1880, thanks mainly to the commercial unification of major parts on the continent, new social as well as cultural and linguistic patterns were emerging, and a cultural unification of central Africa was in progress.

Equally interesting and promising were the political trends in Africa by 1880. The first of these was the trend towards greater and greater centralization. Though some of the existing empires disintegrated during the nineteenth century — typical examples being the Asante and Oyo empires of West Africa and the Luba empire of Central Africa — there were more very large states and empires by 1880 than there had been at the beginning of the century. The Sokoto empire and the Tukulor empire of Masina (the products of the Islamic revolutions to be discussed below) and the empire of Samori Ture, which were all in existence in West Africa by 1880, were much larger in area than any states in existence in that region at the beginning of the century. Other centralized states that had come into existence in Africa by 1880 were Ethiopia, Madagascar, Egypt, Buganda, and Bunyoro. From a series of rival states at the beginning of the nineteenth century, and mainly through military conquests, Ethiopia had become a single centralized state by 1880, while the Imerina kingdom of Madagascar had by that time similarly conquered and incorporated many of the states of the island. In many of these newly created empires and centralized states, some successful attempts were made not only at a cultural renaissance but also at the building of true nation-states by the imposition of the language and culture of the conquering states or dynasties on the conquered ones. This certainly was true of Madagascar, Ethiopia, and Egypt, and to some extent of the Islamic empires of western Africa.

Two completely new and in some ways unique states had also emerged in West Africa by 1880, namely, Sierra Leone and

Liberia. They were founded in 1787 and 1820 from Britain and the United States, respectively, as products of the humanitarian, abolitionist, and racist campaigns of the period. They were to serve as settlements for the liberated slaves in Britain and the Americas as well as for those slaves freed on the high seas by the anti-slave trade naval squadrons. By 1880, both states had been able to absorb some of the surrounding preexisting indigenous states and had developed into true nation-states, each with its own culture and language, Creole and Americo-Liberian. Politically, Liberia had become a sovereign and independent state, while Sierra Leone was still a colony of Britain. Socially and culturally, however, the latter had shown greater originality, initiative, and ingenuity, for the culture and civilization that Sierra Leone had developed by 1880 was not a mere carbon copy of foreign, and in this case American, culture, as those of Liberia were, but rather a very fascinating synthesis of African, Nova Scotian, and British elements. It was undoubtedly the dynamism of this synthesis that enabled its products, the Creoles, to play such a decisive role in the missionary and intellectual revolution in West Africa, as will be discussed below.

Politically, what was even more interesting and significant than the centralizing tendencies were the processes of modernization and constitutional experimentation that had been attempted or were still in progress by 1880 in Africa. It should be emphasized that at least a few African states were not unaware of the many phenomenal scientific, industrial, and technical changes that took place in Europe in the nineteenth century, resulting mainly from the industrial revolution which reached its peak in that century. Nor were they unexposed to some of the products of Europe's industrial capitalism, thanks to the agency of explorers, traders, financiers, missionaries, and shrewd businessmen and companies. Some of them had therefore attempted to modernize by 1880.[6] Thus, Egypt set up her first printing press in 1822; a printing press was built in Portuguese Luanda in 1841; the first modern mines were opened in Algeria in 1843 and in Ghana in the 1870s. Egypt set up many textile and cotton mills, wood mills, glassworks, and a paper mill, all during the reign of Muhammad Ali. Some states, such as Ethiopia and Tunisia, also constructed public works, while nearly all the Barbary states reformed their monetary systems.

Modernization occurred in the military spheres as well. Stimulated by the steady European encroachment, some African states, especially those of North and West Africa, modernized the organization, training, equipment, and recruitment of their armies. Thus, Morocco established an engineering school at Fez to train artillery men, surveyors, and cartographers. Tunisia under Ahmed Bey reorganized her army along Western lines, adopted Western techniques, and set up factories to produce modern guns and other military equipment. Menelik of Ethiopia replaced his unpaid feudal army with a well-equipped army of professional soldiers and built factories to produce cannons and mortars. The great West African general and empire builder Samori Ture reformed and modernized his army and equipped it with some of the latest, most sophisticated weapons of the day. As we shall see later, it was these reforms that enabled Ethiopia to maintain her independence and Samori Ture to resist both the French and the British for so long.

Besides modernizing in these various ways, some African states were experimenting in the constitutional field. As will be discussed below, the number of educated people and ulamas steadily increased throughout the century, and they began to demand a share in the administration of their countries. This led in many African states to a confrontation between the new elite and the old ruling aristocracy, which was resolved in some areas in a violent and militant manner and in other states by peaceful and constitutional solutions. For example, the Fulani jihads of the first half of the nineteenth century, discussed below, could also be described as the militant and violent political solution of the confrontation between the Fulani-educated elite and the traditional Hausa and Mande aristocracies. Likewise, the Dyula rebellions that culminated in the revolt of Samori Ture could be described as a revolt of the educated mercantile Dyula elite against the conservative ruling group. But in other parts of Africa, especially on the west cost, this confrontation was resolved in a constitutional manner, with the educated seeking, not to replace the traditional rulers, but to become their partners.

Nothing illustrates these attempts at constitutional experimentation better than those made by the Fante Confederation formed in Ghana in 1868, the Egba United Board of Management (EUBM) formed in Nigeria in 1865, and the kingdom of the Grebo in Liberia. According to the constitution of the Fante Confederation, adopted in 1871,[7] the officials were to be the king-president, who was "to be elected from the body of kings," and the vice-president, secretary, under secretary, treasurer, and assistant treasurer, "who were to be men of education and position" and were to constitute the Ministry, whose main function was to advise the king-president on all matters. There was to be an Executive Council, to consist of the Ministry (who were to be ex-officio members) "together with such others as may hereafter from time to time be appointed." The Executive Council was to see to the day-to-day affairs of the confederation. There was also to be a Representative Assembly of the confederation, which was to be composed of two representatives from each district, "one educated, the other a chief or the headman," to be appointed by the king or principal chief of the district. This body, which was to be convened by the secretary "as state exigency may require," was to act as the legislative body of the confederation and was to be presided over by the vice-president. The confederation was to hold a general meeting in October each year under the chairmanship of the king-president to "sanction laws, ordinances etc passed by the Representative Assembly," review the business done by the Representative Assembly, and discuss the program of the ensuing year. Finally, there was to be a provincial court, to be presided over by appointed provincial assessers in each district with the Executive Council acting as the final court of appeal.

Particularly relevant and revealing are the objects of the confederation as outlined in the constitution. These were

(i) To promote friendly intercourse between all the kings and chiefs of Fanti, and to unite them for offensive and defensive purposes against their common enemy.

(ii) To direct the labours of the Confederation towards the improvement of the country at large.

(iii) To make good and substantial roads throughout all the interior districts included in the Confederation [and according to article 26, these roads were to connect "various provinces or districts with one another, and with the sea coast," and each road was to be "fifteen feet broad, with good deep gutters on either side"].

(iv) To erect school-houses and establish schools for the education of all children within the Confederation and to obtain the service of efficient school-masters.

(v) To promote agricultural and industrial pursuits, and to endeavor to introduce such new plants as may hereafter become sources of profitable commerce to the country.

(vi) To develop and facilitate the working of the mineral and other resources of the country.

Especially interesting were the provisions made for the promotion of education. There was to be a national school in each district to which would be attached a normal school "for the express purpose of educating and instructing the scholars as carpenters, masons, sawyers, joiners, agriculturists, smiths, architects, builders, etc." Even more interesting was the provision for the establishment of schools to be headed by school mistresses "to train and teach the female sex, and to instruct them in the necessary prerequisites." Though the cost of erecting these schools was to be borne by the confederation, "each king and chief [would] be requested to render all possible aid to facilitate the movement by supplying men and materials." Finally, "in districts where there are Wesleyan schools at present established the kings and chiefs [would] be requested to insist on the daily attendance of children between the ages of eight and fourteen."

These provisions of the constitution of the Fante Confederation are of great significance for four main reasons. First and foremost is the very progressive, modern, and far-sighted nature of the objects and plans of the confederation. This is evident from the plans to construct roads fifteen feet wide, to promote agricultural and industrial pursuits, and "to introduce such new plants as may hereafter become sources of profitable commerce."[8] The second is the great importance attached to the promotion of education — an education not only of a literary but also of a technological and practical nature — as well as the pride of place given to female education and the education of the youth. As Casely Hayford commented on the educational proposals in 1903: "What a far-reaching policy is foreshadowed in the object under discussion. Why, it meant the emergence of the country in two or three generations from a lower order of civilization. It meant providing the country with that incalculable boon, good, intelligent mothers, to guide the growing minds of their offspring."[9] The third significant aspect of the Fante constitution is the spirit of self-help and self-reliance underlying the proposals, a spirit whose importance is only now being acknowledged by the present independent states of Africa. The final and the most innovative is the recognition of the importance of the harmonious cooperation between the educated elite and the traditional rulers for national development.

Had this bold initiative of the Fante Confederation been allowed to be implemented, the course not only of the history of Ghana but indeed of that of the whole of West Africa would have been different. But as Casely Hayford has pointed out, it was not, and as he adds, "What a dream to be frustrated by stupid officialism and red tape."[10] The confederation itself had been killed stone-dead by the British by 1873.

Another interesting constitutional experiment was that of the Egba United Board of Management (EUBM) formed at Abeokuta in Nigeria in 1865. According to Horton, the express purpose of the EUBM was that "of directing the native government, of forwarding civilization, and promoting the spread of Christianity, as well as of protecting the property of European merchants and British subjects."[11] One of its founders and the main leading spirit, G. W. Johnson, an educated Yoruba Creole, or Saro, born in Sierra Leone of Egba parents, stated that it was formed to turn Abeokuta into a "Christian, civilized state independent of foreign leadership" by combining "the authority of the traditional elite with the skills and ideas of westernized Saro."[12] Under the EUBM constitution, the leading traditional ruler, the bashorun, became the president-general, while such executive posts as secretary and treasurer were filled by the educated elite, more evidence of the cooperation between the educated and traditional elites. It is important to note that the EUBM, unlike its contemporary, the Fante Confederation, lasted from 1865 till 1874, and succeeded in introducing such modernizing measures as a postal service to

Lagos, a secular school, sanitary reforms, and above all customs duties on exports with a view to raising revenue for the development of the state.[13]

Such, then, was the political situation in Africa by 1880 — a situation in which the tendency towards greater and greater centralization and cultural renaissance was still in progress, in which attempts at modernization and constitutional experimentation had been and were still being made, and in which the modalities of cooperation between the traditional and new educated elite were being devised. However, it was in the social field that really revolutionary changes had occurred.

The first significant social change was demographic. One of the consequences of the abolition and suppression of the slave trade which has been discussed already must have been a steady increase in population. Indeed, according to recent calculations by Caldwell, the population of Africa increased from about 104 million in 1840 to 120 million in 1880.[14] Whether these figures, based entirely on projections, are accurate or not, it cannot be denied that by 1880, the population of Africa was definitely on the rise, a trend which, as Caldwell has shown, was halted if not reversed as a result partly of the introduction of new diseases and the increased mobility of people into unfamiliar disease environments but mainly as a result of the atrocities and depredations of colonialism, especially between 1880 and 1910. Fortunately, this reversal proved ephemeral, and population growth resumed again after the First World War.

Another interesting aspect of demographic change was the increasing stability of African peoples by 1880. During the first six or seven decades of the nineteenth century Africa had seen a series of mass migrations and movements of peoples. The most phenomenal and dramatic of these were the migrations of the northern Nguni, a Bantu-speaking people who occupied the narrow belt between the Drakensberg Mountains and the Indian Ocean in southern Africa. These migrations were due partly to population pressure but mainly to the political unheavals caused by the activities of some of their chiefs, including Dingiswayo and Shaka, during the first three decades of the century. These migrations, which have become known in history as the *mfecane*, did not lose their momentum until they had swept through the whole of southern, central, and eastern Africa. Another typical example was the migration of the Yoruba from their traditional areas of abode in the savanna regions to the forest and coastal areas of present-day Nigeria, also about the same time. Other migrations involved the Chokwe of Central Africa, the Azande of East Africa, and the Fan of Equatorial Africa. By 1880, most of these dynamic movements had lost their momentum, and most of the people had settled down in their new areas and were busily engaged in adapting their traditional ways of life and institutions to their new ecological and physical conditions. These adaptations and new devices were not only social and cultural but also political. Thus, as Jacob Ajayi and others have shown, the political experiments embarked upon by the Yoruba in their new homes resulted in "Ijaye's military dictatorship, Ibadan's republicanism, Abeokuta's federalism and the confederation of the Ekitiparapo."[15]

But nowhere in the social field had more changes occurred by 1880 than in the field of religion. As a result of a series of jihads in Hausaland under the leadership of Usman dan Fodio in 1804, in Masina under the leadership of Sheikh Ahmadu in 1818, and in the Bambara area under the leadership of Sheikh Umar, or al-Hadj Umar, in 1852[16] — all with the primary aim of spreading and purifying Islam — that Middle Eastern religion, which had been introduced into Africa in the seventh century A.D., had spread into areas hitherto untouched. Thus, by 1880, Islam in the western Sudan had been converted from a religion of the urban and trading centers and court circles into that of the rural areas as well. Moreover, since all three leaders and some of their successors placed a great deal of emphasis on education and learning, on administration in accordance with the Sharia, and on the active participation in the affairs of state by the educated and pious ulamas, not only had the number of the Muslim-educated elite increased and the level of Islamic scholarship and literacy been considerably elevated but Islam had also become greatly strengthened and purified. Above all, since one of the jihad leaders, Sheikh Umar, belonged to the relatively new Tijaniyya order, which appealed more to the ordinary people than to the members of the upper and ruling classes, that order rapidly gained ground in western Sudan and by the end of the period was actively challenging the old, established Qadiriyya order, to which the other two classes belonged. In the 1870s, Islam made further gains as a result of the revolution led by Samori Ture (to be discussed later). The religion had also been strengthened and extended into other parts of Africa, especially into modern eastern Libya, thanks to the activities of the Sanusiyya order, into modern Sudan because of the rise of the Mahdi, and into eastern Africa, especially Buganda, following the activities of the Arab and Swahili traders.

Equally revolutionary and far-reaching in their consequences were the changes that had occurred in the field of Christianity by 1880.[17] At the beginning of the nineteenth century, Christianity was by and large confined to the coastal areas of Africa. There were only three missionary societies operating in the whole of West Africa at the beginning of the nineteenth century — namely, the Society for the Propagation of the Gospel (SPG), the Wesleyan Missionary Society (WMS), and the Glasgow and Scottish Missionary Society (GSMS). Only two were in South Africa by 1800 (the Moravian Mission and the London Missionary Society); there were none in North Africa; and as late as 1850 there was only a single society (the Church Missionary Society) in the whole of East Africa. By 1840, however, the number of societies in West Africa had increased to more than fifteen, that in South Africa to more than eleven by the 1860s, that in East Africa to five by 1877 (including the Roman Catholic missions of the White Fathers and the Holy Ghost Fathers), and that in North Africa to six mostly Catholic missions by 1880. Moreover, these societies were by the end of our period active not only in the coastal areas but also far inland. By the 1860s the societies in South Africa had not only entered the Cape, Natal, and Transvaal areas but had also penetrated as far north as the areas of modern Botswana, Lesotho, Namibia, and Zambia; those in West Africa had reached Kumasi in Ghana, Abeokuta, and the confluence of the Niger and the Benue in modern Nigeria by the

1850s. It should be obvious from the above that by 1880 the missionary impulse in Africa had gathered a revolutionary momentum.

Besides preaching the gospel, converting people to Christianity, and translating the Bible into various African languages, these missionary societies promoted agriculture; taught such skills as carpentry, printing, and tailoring; and promoted trade, literacy, and Western education. All the missionary societies, Protestant as well as Catholic, founded elementary schools, training colleges, and even secondary schools. In West Africa, the CMS, which commenced operations there in 1806, founded the Fourah Bay College as early as 1827, a secondary school for boys and one for girls in 1842, and by 1841 had twenty-one elementary schools in Sierra Leone. The Wesleyans had also established four elementary schools for girls and twenty for boys in Ghana by 1846; in 1876 they founded their first secondary school, the Wesleyan High School, which developed into the present Mfantsipim School. By 1835, the CMS had 4,000 children in its schools in Madagascar, while by 1894, the Protestant missions had a total enrollment of 137,000 pupils in their schools.[18] Even more remarkable was the provision of education in South Africa, where a host of elementary and secondary schools, teacher-training colleges, seminaries, and technical schools had been established by both Protestant and Catholic missionary societies.

By 1880 all the various activities of Christian missionary societies had had a profound impact on African societies. In the first place, the standard of living of the converts had changed, for some were wearing European-style clothes, had gained access to modern medicine, were living in houses built in a modern style, were practicing monogamous marriage, and were feeling contemptuous of their own traditional institutions, their traditional polygamous system of marriage, and their traditional religion. Secondly, African societies had become divided into rival factions — first, into converts and nonconverts or, as they were called in South Africa, the "school" people and the "red" people, with the "school" people further subdivided into Catholic, Methodist, Anglican, Lutheran, and so on.[19] Thus, by 1880 the missionaries had introduced religious pluralism and polarization into Africa, and in areas like Madagascar and Buganda, this caused a great deal of social tension and upheaval.

The greatest social impact on the missionary revolution by 1880, however, was the further stratification of African societies into a relatively small Christian educated elite, particularly in western and southern Africa, and a large traditional and illiterate group. Members of the educated elite were employed as teachers, clergymen, doctors, civil servants, law clerks, journalists, private entrepreneurs, and academics. According to Leo Kuper, 3,448 African students graduated from the Lovedale Missionary Institution in Natal alone between its foundation by the Glasgow Missionary Society in 1841 and 1896; of this number, "over seven hundred were in professional occupations, mostly teachers but including also eight law agents, two law clerks, one physician, and two editors and journalists; almost one hundred were clerks and interpreters, about one hundred and seventy artisans, and over six hundred labourers and farmers."[20] There were many other such institutions in South Africa, and the graduates of these South African schools were to become very active in the mass religious movements of the Bantu in the 1880s and 1890s. They included Tiyo Soga, the first Xhosan to be ordained a minister of the Free Church of Scotland in 1856; Nehemiah Tile, Kenyane, and James M. Awane, all clergymen; and J. T. Javabu, who trained as a teacher, became the first African to pass the matriculation examination in 1883, and played a prominent role in Cape politics between the 1890s and 1910s.[21]

Important as these educated South Africans became, their numbers were extremely small in relation to that of the entire population of the country. Even smaller numerically was the elite that had emerged in eastern and central Africa by 1880, because missionary activities did not really commence in these areas until the 1870s. It was in West Africa that a significant number of educated Africans had emerged by 1880. The country that led in this area was undoubtedly Sierra Leone. Its educated citizens, the Creoles, were mainly responsible for the diffusion of Christianity and Western civilization into the other parts of West Africa. Typical examples of such Creoles are James Africanus Horton, who trained in Britain as a doctor from 1853 to 1859 and joined the West African medical service as a staff assistant-surgeon; Samuel Ajayi Crowther, who was one of the first products of Fourah Bay College and the first African to be ordained as a bishop of the Anglican Church; and James Johnson, the militant intellectual and evangelist.[22] Others were Broughton Davies, who completed his training as a doctor in 1859, and Samuel Lewis, who trained as a barrister and was the first African to be knighted by the queen of England. Among the few intellectuals produced by Liberia was Edward Blyden, who had been born in the West Indies in 1832. In Ghana and Nigeria there had emerged a relatively larger number which by 1880 included, in Ghana, such educated men as J. A. Solomon, J. P. Brown, J. de-Graft Hayford, A. W. Parker, T. Laing, J. H. Brew, and J. M. Sarbah; and in Nigeria, Essien Ukapabio, D. B. Vincent (later known as Majola Agbedi), D. Macaulay, R. B. Blaize, and J. A. Otunba Payne. In Senegal there had emerged educated Creoles like Gaspard Devès, Jean-Jacques Crespin, and Louis Huchard, and in Angola, Canon Antonio José de Nacimento, José de Fontes Pereira, and Joaquim Dias Cordeiro da Mutta.[23]

An equally sizable group had emerged in North Africa in general and in Egypt in particular. Among the latter were the educator Ali Pasha Mubarak; Muhammad and Ahmad al-Qayati, the grandsons of the famous scholar Abd al-Latif al-Qayati of the al-Azhar University and the first of whom, Ahmad, also became a famous sheikh at al-Azhar; Muhammad Ilish (1802–82) and his son Abd al-Rahman Ilish, who also taught at al-Azhar; Hasan al-Idwi (1806–86), another famous ulama; and the last but most famous of them, Muhammad Abduh, a teacher at al-Azhar University, one of whose pupils was Sa ad Zaghul, who was to play such a prominent role in Egyptian politics during the early decades of this century.[24]

While most of these people became clergymen, civil servants, teachers, catechists, journalists, doctors, and lawyers, some of them — especially in West Africa and in the Portuguese areas of Mozambique and Angola — became independent traders and entrepreneurs. Similar social changes had occurred in Madagascar by 1880. It should be clear from the above that by the last decades of the nineteenth century a significant though relatively small educated elite had emerged in Africa in addition to the existing traditional social stratification.

Two other extremely important and interesting social changes, both of them the direct consequences of the emergence of the educated elite, were the development of African religious nationalism, or "Ethiopianism," and a veritable intellectual revolution, especially in South and West Africa. Since these two aspects of the social changes are often ignored by scholars, permit me to dwell a bit on them. Both these unique developments of the latter half of the nineteenth century were the reactions of the African educated elite to the pseudoscientific racist theories of the day in Europe and America, which declared the black man to be an inferior being because of his color. These false racist ideas were given wide publicity as a result of the writings of people like Gobineau, Burton, and Winwood Reade. Most of the European missionaries and administrators were impregnated with these ideas prior to their arrival in Africa. Their consequent discrimination against educated Africans, both in church and state, infuriated many Africans. Some of the educated Africans also grew increasingly resentful of the condemnation of everything African by the missionaries.

This intense feeling of humiliation and indignation among educated Africans gave rise to the religious and political nationalist movement that became known as "Ethiopianism," a term derived from the biblical verse "Ethiopia shall soon stretch out her hands unto God." The principal object of this movement was the establishment of churches which would be controlled by Africans themselves and whose doctrines and rituals would be in tune with African cultures and traditions. It began in West Africa in the 1860s and in South Africa in the 1870s and attained its peak in the 1880s, when the first real breakaway, or Ethiopian, or African independent, church was founded in South Africa by Nehemiah Tile in 1884, and another in West Africa in 1888 by a group of Nigerian church leaders of the Southern Baptist Mission.[25] Ethiopianism rapidly caught on in South Africa, spread

throughout central and eastern Africa, and became a very powerful force throughout Africa and a dynamic instrument of
resistance of colonialism, as will be seen in Chapters 2 and 3.

The educated elite of West Africa did not stop at Ethiopianism,
however. They also took upon themselves the role of refuting the
racist ideas and practices of the day in a series of articles, books,
pamphlets, and speeches. This campaign precipitated the second
unique social revolution of the day, namely, an intellectual
revolution, which, in turn, generated African racial consciousness and identity as well as the ideologies of African personality and Pan-Africanism. In West Africa, the pioneers of this
revolution were John Africanus Horton and Edward Blyden. In
his numerous books and articles, Horton refuted the idea of the
inherent racial inferiority of the black man.[26] In his *West African
Countries and Peoples*, with its significant subtitle *A Vindication
of the African Race*, published as early as 1868, he argued that
the difference in the stages of civilization between whites and
blacks arose "entirely from the influence of external circumstances." He further contended that far from disappearing
from the face of the earth because of racial inferiority, as some
scholars were maintaining, the African people "are a permanent
and enduring people, and the fancies of those who had determined their destruction will go in the same limbo as the now
almost defunct American slavery." Against the proposition that
the black man was incapable of improvement, he argued, in his
preface, that "Africans are not incapable of improvement but . . .
by the assistance of good and able men they are destined to figure
in the course of time, and to take a prominent part in the history
of the civilized world."[27] Again, in the preface to his *Letters on
the Political Conditions of the Gold Coast*, Horton contended:

Rome was not built in a day, the proudest Kingdom in Europe was once
in a state of barbarism perhaps worse than now exists amongst the
tribes chiefly inhabiting the West Coast of Africa; and it is an incon-
trovertible axiom that what has been done can again be done. If
Europe, therefore, has been raised to her present pitch of civilization by
progressive advancement, Africa too, with a guarantee of the civilization of the north, will rise into equal importance.[28]

Besides his condemnation of racism, Horton was also among the first educated Africans to develop and advocate the ideology of Pan-Africanism. According to Shepperson, this ideology was developed during Horton's studies in Britain in answer to the pseudoscientific racist theories.[29] This is borne out by the fact that it was there that he added the name Africanus to his two other names, James Beale. In most of his subsequent writings, he signed himself simply as Africanus Horton.

Edward Blyden, Horton's contemporary, was even more prolific in his writings and more radical in his views. Born in the West Indies, he migrated at an early age to Liberia, where he studied, lived, and worked as a lecturer, politician, and diplomat till his death in 1912 at the age of eighty. In his numerous books and pamphlets and in the many speeches he delivered in Europe and America, he persistently and vehemently condemned the racist theories of the day.[30] In these works, he also advocated Africa for the Africans, Pan-Africanism, African personality, Islam, and polygamy, which were in his view more in keeping with the African personality. He also insisted on the purity and integrity of the black race and therefore condemned mixed marriages, championed Ethiopianism, and above all, preached racial pride. In an article published in 1874, he praised the Mandingo and Fula people, who were Muslim and were independently developing the idea of a national and social order; he concluded:

During all the years, . . . the African race has filled a very humble and subordinate part in the work of human civilization. But the march of events is developing the interesting fact that there is a career before this people which no other people can enter upon. There is a peculiar work for them to accomplish, both in the land of their bondage, and in the land of their fathers, which no other people can achieve. With the present prospects and privileges before this race — with the chances of arduous work, noble suffering, and magnificent achievement before them — I would rather be a member of this race than a Greek in the time of Alexander, a Roman in the Augustin period, or an Anglo-Saxon in the nineteenth century.[31]

In his famous speech to the American Colonization Society in May 1880, Blyden also gave great publicity to the phrase

"Ethiopia shall soon stretch out her hands unto God" and equated "Ethiopian" with "African." Finally, it is now generally agreed that he was the first person to use the term "African personality," in his lecture delivered on 19 May 1893 in Freetown. In this lecture, he described the African race as "a Great Race — great in its vitality, in its power of endurance and its prospect of perpetuity," and pleaded:

It is sad to think that there are some Africans, especially among those who have enjoyed the advantages of foreign training, who are blind to the radical facts of humanity as to say, "Let us do away with the sentiment of Race, let us do away with our African personality and be lost, if possible, in another race. . . . Preach this doctrine as much as you like, no one will do it, for no one *can* do it, for when you have done away with your personality, you have done away with yourselves. . . . The duty of every man, of every race is to contend for its individuality — to keep and develop it. . . . Therefore, honour and love your Race. . . . If you are not yourself, if you surrender your personality, you have nothing left to give to the world.[32]

The last of the leaders of the intellectual revolution to be cited here is the fiery Yoruba-Creole evangelist James Johnson. He condemned racism, advocated "Africa for the Africans," popularized the concept of Ethiopianism in his sermons and writings, and preached Nigerian nationalism. Unlike his contemporary Crowther, he insisted that Africa could be evangelized only by Africans and not by Europeans, since "European missionaries could not identify themselves with African racial ambitions and idiosyncracies."[33] Indeed, he went on to argue that the European presence would prevent the full development of Africans because it would destroy such qualities as "the superior physique, the manly independence, the courage and bravery, the daring and self-reliance, and the readiness to face difficulties" found among Africans who had not come into contact with Europeans.

Similar intellectual activities went on in other parts of Africa, especially in Angola and Egypt. This is evident from the writings of Egyptian scholars such as Sheikh Rifa an Rafe al-Tantawi (1801–73), and from the work in Angola of the writer Joaquim Dias Cordeiro da Mutta and the lawyer and journalist José de

Fontes Pereira.[34] Thus, a real intellectual revolution occurred in West Africa in particular and in Africa in general, its main consequences being the birth of Ethiopianism, Pan-Africanism, and the ideology of African personality, and a generation of pride and confidence in the Negro race. All this prepared the ground for the African independent church movement from the 1880s onwards, which, as will be shown later, resulted in the formation of numerous breakaway African-controlled churches as well as completely new independent churches. This revolution was quite clearly the product both of the missionary educational activities and of the reactions of educated Africans to contemporary racist doctrines.

It should be obvious from the above that on the very eve of the colonial conquest and occupation, Africa was far from being primitive, static, and asleep or in a Hobbesian state of nature. On all fronts — economic, political, social, and even intellectual — Africa was in a mood of change and revolution, accepting new challenges, showing ability at adaptation and modification, fighting back against racist doctrines, and above all changing its economy and politics to suit the socioeconomic realities of the day. It is also clear from the writings of the scholars that the African never thought of himself as being in any way inferior to the European; instead, he believed that, given time, he would become as progressive as the white. Indeed, by 1880 Africans were full of optimism and felt quite ready to face any challenge that was thrown to them. Above all, they seemed determined to defend their sovereignty and way of life.

Nothing illustrates this mood of optimism and readiness better than the very words of the contemporary African rulers themselves. Machemba, king of the Yao in modern Tanzania, told the German commander, Hermann von Wissmann, in 1890:

I have listened to your words but can find no reason why I should obey you — I would rather die first. . . . If it should be friendship that you desire, then I am ready for it, today and always; but to be your subject, that I cannot be. . . . If it should be war you desire, then I am ready, but never to be your subject. . . . I do not fall at your feet, for you are God's creature just as I am . . . I am Sultan here in my land. You are

Sultan there in yours. Yet listen, I do not say to you that you should obey me; for I know that you are free man. . . . As for me, I will not come to you, and if you are strong enough, then come and fetch me.[35]

In 1891, when the British offered protection to Prempeh I of Asante in Ghana, he replied:

The suggestion that Asante in its present state should come and enjoy the protection of Her Majesty the Queen and Empress of India I may say is a matter of very serious consideration, and which I am happy to say we have arrived at this conclusion, that my Kingdom of Asante will never commit itself to any such policy. Asante must remain as of old, at the same time to remain friendly with all white men. I do not write this in a boastful spirit, but in the clear sense of its meaning. . . . the cause of Asante is progressing and there is no reason for any Asante man to feel alarm at the prospects or to believe for a single instant that our cause has been driven back by the events of the past hostilities.[36]

Three years later, in June 1894, after he had been formally installed on the Golden Stool, Prempeh dispatched the following letter to the governor of the Gold Coast:

I pray and beseech my elders, as well as my Gods and the spirits of my ancestors, to assist me, to give me true wisdom and love, to rule and govern my nation, and I beseech you, my good friend, to pray and ask blessings from your God to give me long life and prosperous and peaceful reign, and that my friendship with Her Majesty's Government may be more firm and more closer than hitherto had been done, that bye-gones will be bygones, that Ashanti nation will awake herself as out of sleep, that the hostilities will go away from her, . . . that I shall endeavour to promote peace and tranquility and good order in my Kingdom and to restore its trade, and the happiness and safety of my people generally . . . and thus raise my kingdom of Ashanti to a prosperous, substantial, and steady position as a great farming and trading community such as it has never occupied hitherto, and that the trade between your Protectorate and my kingdom of Ashanti may increase daily to the benefit of all interested in it.[37]

Behanzin, the last king of Dahomey (1889–94), also told the European governments: "God has created Black and White, each to inherit its designated territory. The white man is concerned with commerce and the Black man must trade with the white. Let the Blacks do no harm to the Whites and in the same way the

Whites must do no harm to the Blacks."[38] Hendrik Wittboi, the Nama leader in South West Africa told the Germans in 1894: "The Lord has established various kingdoms in the world. Therefore I know and believe that it is no sin or crime that I should wish to remain the independent chief of my land and people."[39] Makombe Hanga of Mozambique also told a white visitor in 1895: "I see how you White men advance more and more in Africa, on all sides of my country companies are at work. My country will also have to take up these reforms and I am quite prepared to open it up. I should like to have good roads and railways, but I will always remain the Makombe my fathers have been."[40]

In the same year Wobogo, the Moro Naba, or king of the Mossi, told the French captain Restenave: "I know the whites wish to kill me in order to take my country, and yet you claim that they will help me to organise my country. But I find my country good just as it is. I have no need of them. I know what is necessary for me and what I want: I have my own merchants: also, consider yourself fortunate that I do not order your head to be cut off. Go away now, and above all, never come back."[41]

The last and most fascinating piece of evidence I would like to cite here is the moving appeal addressed by Menelik of Ethiopia to Queen Victoria of Great Britain in April 1891. Menelik declared:

I have no intention at all of being an indifferent spectator, if the distant powers hold the idea of dividing up Africa, Ethiopia having been for the past fourteen centuries, an island of Christians in a sea of Pagans.

Since the All-Powerful has protected Ethiopia up until now, I am hopeful that he will keep and enlarge it also in the future, and I do not think for a moment that He will divide Ethiopia among the other Powers.[42]

When, in spite of this appeal, the Italians launched their campaign against Ethiopia with the connivance of Britain and France, Menelik issued his mobilization proclamation in September 1895; here he stated: "Enemies have now come upon us to ruin our country and to change our religion. . . . Our enemies have begun the affair by advancing and digging into the country like moles. With the help of God I will not deliver up my country to them. . . . Today, you who are strong, give me of your strength; and you who are weak, help me by prayer."[43]

It is clear from the very words of the African leaders who were about to face the colonial challenge that they were determined to defend their sovereignty, religion, and traditional way of life but at the same time wanted to cooperate with the Europeans for mutual benefit, and that they were very confident of success.

What, alas, a majority of these African rulers and intellectual leaders had not realized was that by the 1880s and 1890s, the Europe that they were about to encounter was not the same Europe that they had been dealing with since the fifteenth century. It was now a Europe which had witnessed the industrial revolution and was desperately in need of markets as well as raw materials. Nor had they realized that Europe had by that time, again partly as a result of the industrial revolution, dropped her old attitude of free trade and informal political control in favor of one of trade monopoly and direct political and financial control or colonial imperialism. They did not realize that, militarily, Europe had acquired breech-loading rifles and especially the maxim gun and no longer relied on the muzzle-loading muskets or flint guns with which the African armies were armed. Finally, the Africans were not aware that by then Europe had not only the steamship but also the railway and the telegraph, which had greatly facilitated the movement of troops, nor that Europe was medically better prepared and had even acquired an antidote against the malaria which until the 1850s had proved so deadly to Europeans. All this technological superiority of Europe over Africa was summed up beautifully in Hilaire Belloc's famous lines:

Whatever happens we have got
The maxim-gun and they have not.[44]

It is here that our forefathers miscalculated so gravely and with consequences that will be analyzed in the following chapter.

CHAPTER TWO

The Imposition of the Colonial System: Initiatives and Responses

W e have seen in the previous chapter that by as late as 1880, with very few exceptions, Africans were enjoying their sovereignty and were very much in control of their own affairs and destinies. However, within the incredibly short period between 1880 and 1900, all of Africa except Liberia and Ethiopia was seized and occupied by the European imperial powers of Britain, France, Germany, Belgium, Portugal, Spain, and Italy; and Africans were converted from sovereign and royal citizens of their own continent into colonial and dependent subjects. By the 1900s, in place of the numerous African independent states and polities, a completely new and numerically smaller set of some forty artificially created colonies had emerged. These colonies were administered by governors and officials who were appointed by their metropolitan governments and were in no way responsible to their African subjects. By 1910, the colonial system had been firmly imposed on virtually the whole of Africa. In this chapter, I intend to examine this rather unexpected turn of events, which has become known in history as the Scramble for or the Partition of Africa, and more importantly, to analyze the initiatives and reactions of the Africans in the face of this sudden forceful occupation of their land and the imposition of the colonial system.

The circumstances that led to the Scramble for or the Partition of Africa among the imperial European powers have been a matter of contention among historians, both African and European, and have been discussed at length in numerous existing works.[1] I therefore do not intend to devote much time to them. My main concern here is to examine some of the explanations that have hitherto been advanced. The earliest writers, such as Hobson and Lenin, saw the explanation in the rise of the new imperialism in Europe, due primarily to the economic forces operating there during the last three decades of the nineteenth century and, more especially, to the need to look for areas where the surplus capital being generated by these forces could be invested; hence the title of Lenin's book, *Imperialism: The Highest Stage of Capitalism*. Others, especially Robinson and Gallagher, have seen the Scramble as more or less an accidental by-product of the diplomatic confrontations among the major European powers, particularly France and Britain, and argue that the whole Scramble was touched off by the British occupation of Egypt in 1882.

More recently, some European historians, such as Hargreaves and Hopkins, and African historians, such as Asiwaju and Uzoigwe, have attributed the Scramble to a combination of internal African conditions and external European factors. Hopkins, for instance, has argued that in areas where the transition from the slave trade had been successfully made, where incomes had been maintained, and where peace had been established, "an explanation of partition will need to emphasize external pressures, such as mercantile demands and Anglo-French rivalries." On the other hand, in areas "where the indigenous rulers adopted reactionary attitudes, where attempts were made to maintain incomes by predatory means, and where internal conflicts were pronounced," more weight should be placed "on disintegrative forces on the African side of the frontier, though without neglecting external factors."[2] Asiwaju is even more categorical and more persuasive: "The establishment of formal colonial rule must be seen against a background of a major change in what came to be referred to as 'balance of power' in Europe following the rise of Germany, and increasing political instability occasioned by African wars of the nineteenth century which came to threaten peace in the African interior, and consequently European trade on the coast." He has contended that the partition of Africa "cannot become fully intelligible except in terms of the convergence between the new situation in Europe and the prevailing political conditions in particular parts of Africa."[3]

I find these explanations both unconvincing and inadequate, since it was not economic conditions and especially the need to invest surplus capital alone that gave rise to the new imperialist spirit in Europe; as will be shown below, political and social conditions were equally important. The Robinson-Gallagher thesis, which was so fashionable in the early 1960s, has now been proved to be hollow if not totally misconceived. It will be shown presently that as far as West Africa is concerned, the Scramble began in 1879–80, even before the British occupation of Egypt.

Nor do I find the new argument for a mix of Afro-European factors palatable either. Hopkins and his group seem to forget that it was not just during the last three decades of the nineteenth century that indigenous African rulers adopted revolutionary attitudes, that conflicts developed among African states which impeded trade, that conditions in Africa became unstable, or that trade frontiers were disturbed. All these situations had arisen previously in Africa at one time or the other and certainly during the eighteenth century and the early decades of the nineteenth, and yet no partition or scramble occurred. Indeed, it is obvious from Hopkins' own arguments that the parts of Africa that were stable and peaceful did not escape partition any more than those parts that were unstable and rebellious. Furthermore, it was not only those areas of Africa in which Europeans were operating that were partitioned but even those areas in which no European had ever set foot. Finally these scholars seem to be unaware that the European Scramble was not confined to Africa alone but involved the whole of southeastern Asia — Burma, Indochina, Malaya, Java, Sumatra, and the Philippines.[4] In other words, the nature of the internal conditions of Africa and the presence or absence of the slave trade could not and did not precipitate the Scramble, which was in fact a worldwide phenomenon. I believe that the causes of this phenomenon can be found, not in Africa or Southeast Asia, but rather in the congruence of the economic as well as the political and social forces operating in Europe during the last two or three decades of the nineteenth century.

What, then, were these forces? Only a brief answer will be attempted here, since these forces are rather well known. The first and most crucial factor, as the Hobsons and the Lenins have pointed out, was economic. The second half of the nineteenth century was the period during which international trade became increasingly competitive, following the spread of England's industrial capitalism to the other European countries as well as to the United States. The main consequence of this was the emergence of neomercantilism, that is, the abandonment of free trade and the erection of tariff barriers for the protection of the young industries of Europe and America, a step taken by Russia in 1877, Germany in 1879, and France in 1881. These developments created in these industrialized and industrializing countries an urgent need for colonies or areas outside Europe whose markets could become their exclusive monopoly. It became equally urgent to obtain raw materials to feed the new factories; and again, these materials — cotton, palm oil, rubber, peanuts, minerals, and so on — could be obtained or developed in the tropical areas of Africa and Southeast Asia. Indeed, according to Hayes, "what actually started the economic push into the 'Dark Continent' and the sunbaked islands of the Pacific was not so much an overproduction of factory goods in Europe, as an undersupply of raw materials."[5]

The third economic factor, very much emphasized by Lenin, was the need to invest the surplus capital that was being generated by the capitalist system of production. As Lenin contended, "The interests pursued in exporting capital also give an impetus to the conquest of colonies, for in the colonial market it is easier to employ monopoly methods (and sometimes they are the only methods that can be employed) to eliminate competition, to ensure supplies, to secure the necessary 'connections,' etc."[6] This view has been strongly criticized by such scholars as Fieldhouse, mainly on the grounds that the imperial powers did not in fact invest much capital in the colonies that they acquired in Africa, but rather in the United States, Canada, and South America.[7] But Lenin's view seems to me to be valid, first, because even if it is true that not much capital was invested in the colonies after their acquisition, it does not mean that originally the imperial powers did not have the hope of doing so. All that it means is that they grossly miscalculated the investment potential of the colonies. Second, it is a fact that financiers like Von Bleichroeder and Van Hausemann were close associates of Bismarck, and they must have played quite a role in convincing Bismarck to participate in the imperialist marathon race for colonies overseas. Third, there is no doubt that one of the reasons for the British occupation of Egypt in 1882 was to safeguard British investments there. And finally, Jules Ferry, who did so much to push France into the Scramble, is quoted as saying: "Colonies are for rich countries one of the most lucrative methods of investing capital. . . . I say that France, which is glutted with capital and which has exported considerable quantities, has an interest in looking at this side of the question. . . . It is the same as that of outlets for our manufactures."[8]

Besides the strong economic forces, there were also political and social forces precipitating the Scramble that Marxist-Leninists tend to ignore. The most important of these political factors was an exaggerated spirit of nationalism in Europe following the unification of both Germany and Italy and especially after Germany's defeat of France in 1871. With the emergence of a strong national consciousness, nations began to think not only of their power and progress but also of their prestige, greatness, and security. Unfortunately, in Europe of the last decades of the nineteenth century, the number of overseas colonies a nation possessed became a measure or symbol of its prestige and greatness, just as dispatching a satellite into earth orbit is today. Portugal (then regarded as "the sick man of Europe"), Germany, and later Italy all rushed for colonies overseas to prove that they had acquired a place in the sun, and France did so to prove that she was still a great power despite her humiliating defeat by Germany in 1871.

The main social condition contributing to the rise of the new imperialism was the need to acquire colonies where the surplus labor produced by the industrial capitalist system as well as the large numbers of the unemployed could be settled without losing their nationality or severing their links with their mother country. It was partly to undertake such colonization that a number of colonization societies emerged in Europe, especially in Germany and Italy, during the period under review, and some of these societies did exert pressure on their governments to acquire colonies.

Thus, it was the conjunction of all these forces in Europe in the 1880s, and not any conditions in either Africa or Asia, that accounts for the Scramble for Africa as well as for Asia during the last two decades of the nineteenth century. The most important and decisive of those forces were definitely economic. I entirely agree with the view of Arnold that "the 'New' or 'Economic' Imperialism that dominated international politics in the 1880s can, therefore, be seen primarily in terms of the intensification of competition between the principal industrial states for a share of the world's markets. . . . It was an almost hysterical reaction to the crisis in industrial capitalism, feeding on a fear that the economic and hence political future of an industrial country rested on the exclusive control of markets and raw materials."[9]

When, then, did this virtually inevitable race for colonies in Africa begin? Recent research has now conclusively proved that it did not begin in 1882 or 1884, as has hitherto been supposed, but rather in 1879, when three starting shots were fired.[10] The first was the dispatch of three French missions to explore routes for the trans-Saharan railway; the second was the appointment of Major Gustave Borgnis-Desbordes as the commander of the Upper Senegal to push French imperial interests inland; the third was the dispatch in the same year, both by King Leopold of Belgium and by the French, of Stanley and de Brazza, respectively, to conclude treaties with the rulers of the Congo basin. This sudden intrusion of Stanley and de Brazza greatly alarmed Portugal and Britain which had hitherto regarded that area as their exclusive preserve, and they therefore began their counter-moves. Britain became even more alarmed when France annexed Port Novo and Little Popo in 1883 and began her activities on the Niger. To checkmate both the French and Leopold, Britain backed Portugal on the Congo issue, while to safeguard her interests in the Bight of Benin and Biafra, now threatened by the French moves, she sent Hewett to declare a protectorate over the Oil Rivers and the Cameroons in May 1884. The British were shocked to find that Germany, which had hitherto not been reckoned with, had already planted her flag in Togo and the Cameroons in June 1884.[11] With the entry of Germany, the Scramble was well and truly on.

It was with a view of formulating rules for the conduct of the ongoing race in order, particularly, to avoid any armed confrontations among the imperial powers that an international conference was held in Berlin under the chairmanship of Bismarck, the chancellor of Germany.[12] This Berlin Conference was attended by every Western nation except Switzerland and the United States but not by even a single African state, and it lasted from 15 November 1884 to 31 January 1885. Four main rules were agreed upon at the conference.[13] The first was that before any power claimed an area, it should inform the other signatory powers so that any who deemed it necessary could make a counterclaim. The second was that all such claims should be followed by annexation and effective occupation before they could be accepted as valid. The third was that treaties signed with African rulers were to be considered as legitimate titles to sovereignty. The fourth rule was that each power could extend its coastal possessions inland to some extent and claim spheres of influence. Finally, it was agreed that there was to be freedom of navigation on the Congo and the Niger rivers. All these rules were embodied in the Berlin Act, ratified on 26 February 1885. This act, then, cleared the last main hurdle in the way of the Scramble or Partition, that of a possible military conflict between the imperialists, and European occupation continued with renewed vim and vigor from then on. It should be emphasized that the Berlin Conference did not start the Scramble but merely accelerated a race that was already in progress. Italy belatedly entered this race with her occupation of the Eritrean coast in 1889.

The Scramble was carried on in three stages. The first stage was the conclusion of a treaty between an African ruler and a European imperial power under which the former was usually accorded protection and undertook not to enter into any treaty relation with another European power, while the latter was granted certain exclusive trading and other rights. Thus, between 1880 and 1895, the British concluded treaties with many rulers in northern Ghana and in Yorubaland and Benin in Nigeria, and, as may be recalled, offered protection to the king of Asante. During the same period the French signed treaties with Ahmadu of the Tukulor empire, with Samori Ture and the king of Dahomey, and with some of the rulers of the Congo basin. Some of these treaties were in fact forced on the Africans, a typical example being the treaties between the British East Africa Company and Buganda in 1890 and 1892.

The second stage was the signing of bilateral treaties between the imperial powers usually based on the earlier treaties of protection which defined their spheres of interest and delimited their boundaries.[14] Thus, by the Anglo-German Treaty of 1890, Germany recognized British claims to Zanzibar, Kenya, Uganda, Northern Rhodesia, Bechuanaland, and eastern Nigeria; the Anglo-French Treaty of the same year laid down the western boundary of Nigeria while Britain recognized French claims to Madagascar. The Franco-Portuguese Treaty of 1886 and the German-Portuguese Treaty of 1891 accepted Portugal's supremacy in Angola and Mozambique and delimited Britain's sphere in central Africa. It should be emphasized that these European bilateral treaties were concluded without any consultations whatsoever with the African states.

The third and final stage was that of the European conquest and occupation of their spheres. Though this has been described in typical Eurocentric terms as the phase of pacification, it was in fact the most bloody and the most brutal of all the stages of the Scramble from the Afrocentric standpoint. Thus, from 1885 the French began their invasions and occupations in the western Sudan and conquered Cayor in 1886 and the Soninke empire of Samori in 1898.[15] The British also moved in troops and occupied Asante in 1896, Ijebu in 1892, Benin in 1897, the Sokoto empire between 1900 and 1904, and Sudan between 1896 and 1899, while the Germans conquered and occupied what became known as German East Africa between 1888 and 1907. By 1910, with the exception of a few areas such as eastern Libya, the Rif areas, and parts of the Sahara, the European occupation of Africa had been completed, and the colonial system had been imposed.

The final question, then, and the one with which this chapter is really concerned, is what the initiatives and reactions of the

Africans were in the face of all these European imperialist activities during the last two decades of the nineteenth century. Until the 1960s, the African spectrum of the Scramble or Partition was ignored in African historiography. At the epoch-making International Congress of African Historians held at the then University College of Dar-es-Salaam in October 1965 on the topic "Emerging Themes of African History," the Russian historian A. B. Davidson, in his key-note address, stated:

We can say that for the time being the studying of the question of the struggle of African people is still in embryo. As a matter of fact historians have not really raised yet the problems of Africans' resistance to colonialism. It is to be supposed that many rebellions are not yet known; that historians have not discovered them yet. . . . It is not discovered yet what were the motive forces of rebellion, how they were organised, why rebels undertook one or another action, what was the inner communication between different events linked with a rebellion. About other forms of resistance we know even less than about armed rebellion.[16]

As Davidson predicted, a great deal has indeed been learned about the theme in question since then. Many, indeed numerous, rebellions have been "discovered," and other forms of reactions have been dug up from various archives. It is quite evident from this rapidly accumulating evidence that Africans reacted differently to the creeping European imperialism and that the initiatives and responses of each state or group were very much influenced by its political and social structure, its level of contact with Europeans and Islamic influences, the prevailing political and environmental conditions at the time, and, finally, the methods adopted by the European imperialists to establish their control over that group. Secondly, as has been seen already, the Scramble was accomplished in three different stages, and each stage generated its own type of reactions.

It was pointed out in the first chapter that by 1880 African society had crystallized into two main groups. These were the relatively small educated and professional elite and the overwhelmingly large traditional and illiterate group. The educated elite was further divided into the Christian subgroup, found mainly in the coastal areas, and the Muslim subgroup, found in the coastal as well as the interior parts of the continent, especially in eastern and northern Africa. As one would expect, the attitudes of the educated Christian Africans differed markedly from those of the traditional group as well as from the educated Muslim Africans. It is quite clear from the available evidence that a majority of the Christians warmly welcomed the encroaching colonial imperialism. In many areas in South, Central, and West Africa, it was they together with their white missionaries who put pressure on both the local administration and the metropolitan governments to annex or establish protectorates over certain areas before they were acquired by other foreign European powers. The newspapers of Ghana and Sierra Leone of the 1870s and 1880s, for instance, are full of appeals to the British government to annex the hinterlands of the colonies.[17] Even Blyden, that great African cultural nationalist and Pan-Africanist, repeatedly urged the British in the 1880s and 1890s to occupy the whole of West Africa and thereby exclude the French and the Germans. After the Partition he declared: "Our country has been partitioned, in the order . . . of providence, by the European powers, and I am sure that, in spite of what has happened, or is now happening or may yet happen, this partition has been permitted for the ultimate good of the people and for the benefit of humanity."[18]

That these educated Christian Africans should have reacted in this way should not surprise us. With very few exceptions, they had been made to believe that Africa could be civilized only through "introducing Christianity, education, capitalism, industrialization and the Protestant work ethic," and they saw the colonial conquest and occupation as the most effective way of introducing all these into Africa.[19] The educated Muslims, on the other hand, were opposed to the colonial occupation for reasons that should also be obvious. As Crowder has pointed out, "For Muslim societies of West Africa the imposition of white rule meant submission to the infidel, which was intolerable to any good Muslim."[20]

What is more important are the reactions of the overwhelming majority of the Africans, namely, the traditional and illiterate group. During the first stage — that is, the stage of treaty-making between African rulers and the Europeans — the attitude of these Africans was on the whole very friendly and accommodating. Indeed, it would appear that only a very few of them rejected these treaties of trade, friendship, and protection; among them were Prempeh I of Asante and Cetshwayo, King of the Zulu. This initially friendly reaction was undoubtedly due to a number of considerations. In the first place, the African rulers were initially regarded as the equals of their European counterparts and were treated with every respect and decorum by the European envoys and negotiators. Secondly, unlike Prempeh, who was so confident of his own ability to handle the political situation with which he was confronted, many of the African rulers did in fact need some such protection and assistance, either against other European powers or other, more powerful African rivals or even against their own subjects. Indeed, in some cases it was the African kings themselves who took the initiative and invited the Europeans in. It was King Mbandzeni of the Swazi, for instance, who asked for British protection against the Boers and the European concessionaries; the emir of Nupe similarly invited the French to form an alliance with him against the British Royal Niger Company. The African rulers also wanted not only the protection but also the trade that was envisaged. After the signing of the treaty of friendship and freedom of trade with the British on 8 July 1892, the king of Daboya in northern Ghana gave the following message to the British envoy to be delivered to the governor of the Gold Coast:

Tell my friend, the Governor of Accra, I like his friendship, I like a man who is not a foolish man. I like a man who is truthful. Tell my friend I like my country to be quiet and secure; I want to keep off all my enemies and none to be able to stand before me. Then the men, women, and everybody can get road to the beach. . . . When one is coming to tell me whether the treaty I have made stands good [i.e., ratified], tell my friend to send me a cane messenger stick like the one which you hold. Let plenty guns, flint, powder and cloth, and every kind of cost goods be sent here for sale. I want a rare magnificent cloth myself to put on. Tell him also to send for sale here those short small guns firing many times [revolvers], a telescope like the one with which you have observed the moon all night, and ascertained distant objects by day and above all I will buy iron clothes [i.e., coat of arms] from my friend at any cost.[21]

These negotiations were also often preceded by lavish presents and especially bottles — if not cases — of liquor, which never failed to smooth the movement of the wheels of diplomacy.

Finally, there is no doubt that in some cases, the African rulers were deceived or misled into signing treaties which contained clauses whose full meaning and implications were not explained or even made known to them. That such tricks were played was admitted even by Lugard, that overenthusiastic British imperialist agent, himself. About the treaty between the British East African Company and Kabaka Mwanga of Buganda in 1892, he noted in his diary:

No man if he understood would sign it, and to say that a savage chief has been told that he cedes all rights to the company in exchange for nothing is an obvious untruth. If he had been told that the Company will protect him against his enemies, and share in his wars as an ally, he has been told a lie, for the Company have no idea of doing any such thing and no force to do it with if they wished.[22]

As is well known, Menelik, the emperor of Ethiopia, and Lobengula, king of the Ndebele, were similarly tricked into signing the Treaty of Wuchale and the Rudd concession, respectively, in 1889.

Since the second stage of the Scramble, that of the bilateral European treaties, took place in Europe without the knowledge or participation of the Africans themselves, one would not expect any reactions. It was during the third stage, when, armed with these treaties of trade and protection as well as the bilateral treaties, the European imperial armies moved in to conquer and occupy territories, that the Africans rulers realized the full implications of the race in progress. Particularly astounded and infuriated were those rulers such as Menelik and Lobengula who found that they had either been tricked into signing treaties in which they supposedly had surrendered all or part of their sovereignty or land.[23] Unlike their educated Christian subjects, they did not welcome these invaders but, rather, resorted to a number of strategies with the primary objective of safeguarding their sovereignty.

What, then, were these strategies? The available evidence indicates that Africans devised three main strategies during the period under review. These were submission, alliance, and confrontation. Confrontation was of two varieties: peaceful confrontation or diplomacy, and violent or armed confrontation, which involved differing tactics — open warfare, sieges, guerilla warfare, and scorched-earth practices. It is equally clear from the accumulating data that some African rulers and leaders stuck to one strategy throughout, while several others used a combination of these strategies. Thus, some submitted only to rise up again; many combined diplomacy with armed confrontation; others resorted to alliance at one time and armed confrontation at another. It is this variation in strategies that makes the classification of African rulers into resisters and so-called collaborators so prevalent in the 1960s and 1970s very misleading and, indeed, erroneous. Let us then look at each of these strategies.

It is a fact that some African rulers and leaders readily submitted to the European invaders. In French West Africa, M'backe of Sine and Guedel M'bodj of Salum in the region of Senegambia submitted. So did nearly all the Yoruba states of Nigeria, including Abeokuta, Ibadan, Oyo, Ekiti, and Ijesa. In southern Africa, the rulers of the Ngwato, Lozi, Sotho, Tswana, and Swazi also surrendered readily. This particular strategy was not without its justification. These rulers readily submitted either because they became aware of the futility and cost of confronting the imperialists or, more commonly still, because they themselves urgently needed European protection. Many of the Yoruba states submitted because of the lesson they derived from the disastrous defeat inflicted on one of them, Ijebu, which had dared to oppose the British.[24] Though the white missionaries did exert pressure on some of the South African states, there is no doubt that those small states in the heart of South Africa were facing grave danger of being subjugated either by the Zulu or the Ndebele or the Boers and saw the British really as saviors. Indeed, it was Kgama, the king of the Ngwato, who wrote to the "Great Queen of the

English people" to ask for her protection.²⁵ This strategy paid off in the end, legally at least, because while most of these acquiescing states — Swaziland, Bechuanaland, and Nyasaland — became only protectorates, those states whose rulers opted for confrontation became, as we shall see below, full-fledged colonies.

The second main strategy adopted, one often later dropped in favor of the third strategy, was that of alliance. In central Africa, the Inhambane Tonga and the Sena allied with the Portuguese against their Shangaan and Barue rulers. In the Congo Free State, Tippu Tip, the Swahili-Arab trader, and the sons of Msiri, the Nyamwezi trader, who had created huge empires for themselves in central Africa during the second half of the nineteenth century, initially allied with the Belgians. In southern and central Africa, the Alubi, Mpondomise, Bhaca, Senga, and Njanja also allied with the British against their more powerful neighbors, the Zulu, Ndebele, Bemba, Yao, or Nguni, who had been raiding them or extorting tributes from them. In East Africa, Waiyaki, leader of the Masai, teamed up with the British against the Kikuyu among whom Waiyaki had settled. King Mumia of the Wanga in western Kenya allied with the British, as he thought that he could use them to extend his influence over the whole of western Kenya and defeat his old enemies, the Iteso and the Luo, while the British were also expecting him to assist them to achieve the same end. Of course, it was the British who won in the end.

In Tanganyika, the Marealle, the Kibonga, and the Usambara allied with the Germans to defeat their enemies. In Buganda, while King Kabarega opposed the British, as will be seen below, some of the Baganda allied with the British, especially Kakunguru and his followers, and it was Kakunguru who captured Kabarega. It was because of this alliance that the Baganda later became such important colonial agents of the British in Uganda. In West Africa, Tieba, the king of Sikasso in the northern Ivory Coast; Bokar Saada, the ruler of Bundu in the Senegambia; and Tofa, the king of Porto Novo in Dahomey, allied with the French. When Ahmadu of the Tukulor empire succeeded his father in 1864, he decided on a policy of alliance with the French, and he stuck to this policy until the very last two years of his reign, 1890 and 1891.²⁶

I believe enough illustrations have been cited to show that some African rulers did form alliances with the European powers. These are the rulers who were classified as collaborators by many historians in the 1960s and 1970s and were lauded to the skies as having been long-sighted and progressive, while those who adopted the strategy of militant confrontation were condemned as being romantic, short-sighted, and reactionary. To quote two of these historians:

If these were far-sighted and well-informed, and more particularly if they had access to foreign advisers such as missionaries or traders, they might well understand that nothing was to be gained by resistance, and much by negotiation. If they were short-sighted, less fortunate, or less well-advised, they would see their traditional enemies siding with the invader and would themselves assume an attitude of resistance, which could all too easily end in military defeat, the deposition of chiefs, the loss of land to the native allies of the occupying power, possibly even to the political fragmentation of the society or state. . . . As with the slave trade in earlier times, there were gainers as well as losers, and both were found within the confines of every colonial territory.[27]

I find the term *collaborator* highly objectionable partly because it is inaccurate and partly because it is Eurocentric and derogatory.[28] Ever since World War II, the term *collaborator* has assumed very pejorative connotations, and its use should therefore be avoided as much as possible. In any case, it is totally wrong in the African context. A collaborator is surely somebody who sacrifices the interests of his nation for his own selfish ends. But what these African rulers sought to achieve was not their own selfish ends but in fact the very sovereignty of their state, and what they saw themselves as doing was not collaborating but rather allying with the incoming invaders to achieve this national end. Let us look in detail at the cases of two of these so-called collaborators — that of Tofa of Porto Novo and that of Sheikh Ahmadu of the Tukulor empire — to highlight the issues at stake.

Tofa, the king of Porto Novo and a vassal of the king of Dahomey, has been cited as a typical example of a collaborator by some historians. But was he? At the time that the French appeared on the coast of Dahomey, Tofa was facing threats to his sovereignty from all sides — from the English on the coast, from the Fon kings in the interior, and from the Yoruba to the north-east.[29] He therefore must have seen the arrival of the French as providential and saw himself as using them to end all those threats and even to regain his independence from the Fon kings at Abomey.

As we have noted, Sheikh Ahmadu of the Tukulor empire stuck to his policy of alliance with the French till the last two years of his reign. However, only those unaware of the problems confronting him at the time of his accession and throughout his reign would call him a collaborator. Soon after his accession, Ahmadu found himself facing three challenges: from his own brothers, who were contesting his authority; from his subjects and vassals, namely the Bambara, Mandinka, Fulbe, and others; and from the French to the west. To make matters worse, the military strength of the empire had been considerably weakened as a result of the incessant wars of his father and founder of the empire, al-Hadj Umar. His concerns, then, must have been, first to consolidate his position and, second, to ensure the continued sovereign existence of the empire. To achieve both ends, he obviously needed arms and ammunition to increase the military power of the state and financial resources to meet his military and administrative expenses. He must have seen alliance or coopera-tion with the French as the obvious solution. It is not surprising, then, that he readily agreed to negotiations with the French, which resulted in the treaty of 1878. Under this treaty, the French were allowed to trade in his empire in return for the supply of some arms and ammunition and for the recognition of Ahmadu's authority.

Though the French did not ratify this treaty and even con-tinued to assist some of his rebel subjects, Ahmadu continued to cooperate with the French because that temporary understanding enabled him to quell the rebellions of his brothers and those in Segu and Kaarta by the late 1870s. In 1880, he once again readily agreed to open negotiations with the French, who were them-selves about to launch a major invasion for the conquest of the Upper Senegambia region and therefore needed the neutrality if not the support of Ahmadu. Under the terms of this treaty, the Treaty of Mango, Ahmadu agreed to allow the French to construct and maintain trade routes throughout his empire and to build and sail steamboats on the Niger. For their part, the French undertook to recognize the sovereignty of the empire, never to invade Ahmadu's territory, and never to build any fortification in it. Above all, the French agreed to give Ahmadu four field guns and 1,000 rifles and to pay a yearly rent of 200 rifles, 200 barrels of powder, 200 artillery shells, and 50,000 flints.[30]

This treaty was, on the face of it, a great diplomatic victory for Ahmadu, and had it been ratified and faithfully implemented by both sides, the Tukulor empire would have survived. But even the French officer who led the negotiations, Captain Gallieni, had no intention of implementing it, nor was it ever ratified by the French government. In fact, the treaty was followed by an invasion of the Tukulor empire by the French in 1881, and by 1883 they had occupied Bamako, on the Niger. But even this invasion did not convince Ahmadu of the futility of his strategy, for in May 1887, he again agreed to negotiate with the French. The result was the Treaty of Gori, signed in 1887. Under this treaty, Ahmadu now changed his strategy to one of submission by agreeing to place his empire under the nominal protection of the French, while the French on their part pledged not to invade his territories and to lift the ban that they had placed on the purchase of arms by Ahmadu.

The interesting issue here is why the French needed the alliance of Ahmadu at this time and why Ahmadu agreed to it. Between 1885 and 1888 the French were engaged in the suppression of the rebellion of Mamadou Lamine, and they were therefore extremely anxious to prevent any alliance between Ahmadu and Mamadou. For his part, Ahmadu was still engaged in overpowering his brothers, and he therefore also urgently needed the support of the French. It is not surprising then that both agreed to the conclusion of another treaty.

Even though this treaty was humiliating to Ahmadu, involving as it did a compromise on his hitherto entrenched position of the absolute sovereignty of his empire, the French did not observe it. On the contrary, they assumed the offensive against him in 1889 with an attack on the Tukulor fortress of Kundian. The French did so now because having suppressed Mamadou Lamine's rebellion and having signed a treaty with Samori in 1887, which will be discussed presently, they no longer needed Ahmadu's alliance. It was at this point that Ahmadu abandoned his other strategies and resorted to military confrontation. His forces bravely defended the fortress and replied to the French bombardment with continued musket-fire. When the fortress was captured, they courageously fought on, even from house to house, until most of them died "with their weapons in their hands." The French pressed on and captured the capital of the empire, thanks to their two 95-mm field guns with a hundred of the latest mellinite shells. Ahmadu and his soldiers refused to surrender even after the capture of their capital but continued to resist until the final defeat at the hard-fought battle at Kori-kori in January 1891. After this defeat, Ahmadu went into exile in Hausaland rather than surrender, still maintaining, according to Saint-Martin, an attitude of "uncompromising independence" toward the French.[31]

It should be obvious from the above analysis, then, that only historians who are unaware of the political problems confronting Ahmadu and Tofa or who interpret these facts from the Eurocentric standpoint would describe Tofa and Ahmadu as collaborators. The evidence makes clear that an overwhelming majority of those who formed these alliances did so, not to further the interests of the European imperialists or even to gain their own selfish ends, but to preserve the sovereignty and independence of their states. In any case, since most of them abandoned the strategy of alliance for that of submission or, more usually, for that of militant confrontation, this dichotomy between collaborators and resisters is clearly a figment of the imagination of these Eurocentric historians.

The third and final strategy Africans resorted to in the face of European colonial imperialist aggression and occupation was confrontation. As already indicated, there were two variants of this strategy, the armed or militant form and the peaceful or diplomatic form. It was once very widely believed that only African peoples with centralized systems of government — that is, those who lived in states under kings or other rulers — adopted the militant option. But it has now been conclusively proved that this is

completely false, and that, on the contrary, some of those peoples without centralized systems of government not only also
chose this option but that they often held out even longer than resisters with centralized governments.[32]

Relatively few African rulers decided to stick to diplomacy
alone as a means of maintaining their independence. Among
those few were Jaja of Opobo in the Niger delta and Prempeh I of
Asante in Ghana. We have already noted that Prempeh was one
of the few African rulers to turn down the offer of protection by
the British in 1891. In February 1894, the British governor, after
having received instructions from London, submitted a new set
of proposals to Prempeh in which the British offered to station a
resident in Kumasi "to be consulted on such matters as those re-
lating to war and peace and in return to pay annual stipends to
the King, Queen and the leading chiefs." At the meeting of the
Confederacy Council in June 1894, at which Prempeh was formally installed as the Asantehen, the council also decided once
again to reject the British offer of protectorate status in favor of
other arrangements which would ensure the independence of
Asante. As Albert Owusu Ansa, one of the few educated Asante
advisers of Prempeh, wrote to the governor after the meeting,
"As my countrymen are desirous of continuing their independence, I beg here strongly to suggest to your Excellency that it is
essential that the [British] government ought now to formally
acknowledge Ashanti as an independent native empire, or in
other words engagements entered into with her similar to the understanding now existing between Her Majesty's Government
and the Ameer of Afghanistan by which annexation by any
power is rendered impossible."[33]

Convinced that further negotiations with the governor would
not be fruitful, the council accepted the advice of John Owusu
Ansa, another educated Asante and brother of Albert, that an
embassy should be sent to London to discuss the matter directly
with the British government. This embassy, made up of six people under the leadership of John Owusu Ansa, was to see the
queen of England to "lay before your Majesty certain diverse
matters affecting the good estate of our kingdom." It was, in particular, to discuss the terms under which a resident would be sta-

tioned in Kumasi, since "it is understood that unless the terms of the appointments be carefully defined, the appearance of Resident in Coomassie is likely to be followed at an early date by the definite conversion of the country into a British Protectorate."[34]

The mission left Cape Coast for England on 3 April 1895, against the advice of the governor, and landed at Liverpool on the twenty-fourth. Though it remained in England till December 1895, not only did the British government refuse to receive the mission but while the mission was still there decided, for reasons to be discussed below, to send an expedition against Asante and appointed Captain Scott as its commander. This expedition entered Kumasi in January 1896 without meeting any resistance, since in spite of the clamor of his captains for war, Prempeh had decided not to fight the British. Prempeh made this rather unexpected and most uncharacteristic decision on the grounds, as he himself later explained, that since it was the British who assisted him in winning the throne and played a great part in bringing about peace in Asante, "I am not prepared to fight the British troops in spite I am to be captured by them — secondly, I would rather surrender to secure the lives and tranquility of my people and countrymen."[35] Although Prempeh submitted without a fight, he, his mother, father, and brother and many of the leading Asante chiefs were all arrested and deported, first to Freetown in Sierra Leone and from there to the Seychelles Islands in 1900. Most of the chiefs died there, and Prempeh was not repatriated by the British until 1924.

But if Prempeh and a few other African rulers resorted to diplomacy, an overwhelming majority of the Africans adopted the military option, either in isolation or in combination with diplomacy. The purely military option was more commonly applied in West Africa, the Nile Valley, and North Africa than in the other parts of Africa. This, surely, must have been partly because those areas were predominantly Muslim and partly because those areas fell mainly to the French, who used more militant than peaceful, diplomatic methods in their occupation of these areas.

Let us, then, make a survey of the African rulers and leaders who chose this option either in its pure or combined form and later discuss some of them in detail by way of illustration.[36] In southern Africa, the major African nations of the area—the Zulu, Ndebele (in modern Zimbabwe), Bemba (in Zambia), and Yao (in Malawi)—chose confrontation, though most of their kings, including Cetshwayo of the Zulu and Lobengula of the Ndebele, relied on diplomacy for quite a long time before resorting to arms. But it was not the large centralized states alone which fought against the British. Some small groups — such as the Barwe, Mangwende, Makoni, Mutasa, and the Xosa paramountcies of the area—also chose armed confrontation. In central Africa, the Yao, Makua, Yeke, Chikunda, Ovimbundu, Chokwe, Lunda, Chewa, Humbe, Bihe, Shangaan, and Nguni, mostly of Angola and Mozambique, all forcefully opposed the Portuguese, Belgians, and British; and some of their kings committed suicide, as did the Chewa leader Mwase Kasungu in 1896, rather than capitulate to the British. Many of the rulers, such as Gungunyane of the Shangaan, the Barue royal family, and Bemba, resorted to arms only after years of diplomatic maneuvering with the imperialists.

In East Africa, the Nandi, part of the Masai, the Mazrui family, and the Akamba (all of Kenya), the Mbunga, Makonde, Hehe, and the Swahili of the coast of Tanzania under Abushiri also forcefully resisted the British and the Germans. In fact, Abushiri and his forces attacked the Germans in August 1888 and succeeded in driving them from the coastal towns except Bagamoyo and Dar es Salaam. Later, however, the German government brought in large reinforcements which succeeded in defeating and capturing Abushiri, whom they hanged in December 1899. The leader of the Hehe, Nkwana, fought against the Germans between 1891 and 1894 and committed suicide rather than surrender or be captured. In Uganda, Kabarega of Bunyoro and Mwanga of Buganda used diplomacy as well as force to defend their sovereignty from 1891 till 1899, when they were both captured by the British. They were taken to Kisimayu, where Mwanga died in 1903, while Kabarega was deported to the Seychelles Islands to join Prempeh and his group.

In northern and northeastern Africa, the stand of the Africans in defense of their sovereignty and religion was the fiercest, bloodiest, and most protracted. The Egyptians, under the gallant leadership of Colonel Ahmad Urabi, rose up against the British invasion of their country in 1882. In their defense of Alexandria alone, in July 1882, they lost about 2,000 men. In the Sudan, under the Mahdi, Muhammad Ahmad Ibn Abdullah, and his successor, Khalifa Abudullah, the Sudanese fought for their sovereignty first against the Turco-Egyptian regime and then against the British from 1881 till 1899. Some of these battles were very bloody. At the battle of Atbara in April 1898 between the British forces under Kitchener and the Sudanese, 3,000 Sudanese were killed and over 4,000 were wounded. At the decisive battle of Karari, near Omdurman, on 2 September 1899, nearly 11,000 Sudanese were killed and 1,600 wounded. The final confrontation took place at the battle of Umm Diwaykrat on 22 November 1899, during which many of the Mahdist generals and leaders were killed, among whom was the Khalifa himself. This battle marked the end of Sudanese attempts to defend their sovereignty as well as the end of the Mahdist state.

In Southern Sudan, the Nuer and especially the Azande under their king, Yambio, first employed diplomatic measures by playing the British and the Belgians against each other and then resorted to arms to maintain their independence until January 1905, when Yambio was defeated and imprisoned.

Equally determined and protracted, though unsuccessful, was the Somalis' defense of their lands and sovereignty against the quadruple assault of the British, Italians, French, and Ethiopians. Like the peoples of Southern Sudan, they first used diplomacy to play one imperial power against the other and then resorted to arms. The Somalis held out from 1884 until 1897, when the imperialist occupation of Somaliland was completed. It was in Ethiopia, the last state in this region, that a spirited and this time very successful defense was staged, as will be seen below.

The peoples and rulers of the Barbary states of Libya, Tunis, and Morocco similarly stood up against the French, Italians, and Spaniards. In Tunisia, while the Bey readily submitted to the French and accepted a protectorate status in May 1881, his people in the interior and especially those of the religious capital, Kayruwan, rose up in defense of their land, and it took two French expeditions to overcome this opposition. The Berber of

Tuat in southern Morocco also opposed the French, and it was only after some bloody battles, including the one at Char in December 1899 and another at Talmin in March 1901, that the French could occupy the area. In the areas of Trarza and Brakna, Sheikh Ma'al-Aynayn led the people in a series of battles against the French invaders during which they killed the French leader Xavier Coppolani in April 1905 in his camp at Tidjikdja and repulsed the French army under Colonel Gouraud at al-Mugnam on 16 June 1908. From here Sheikh Ma'al-Aynayn retreated into the Sakiyat al Kamra, from whence his forces continued to harass the French and the Spaniards until 1933. Further south, the people of the Rif under the inspired leadership of Sheikh Ameriyan held out against the Spaniards from 1909 till 1926. Even more spirited and protracted was the defense of the people of Libya against the Italians; under their famous leaders Sayyid Ahmad al-Sharif al-Sanusi and Umar al-Mukhar, the Libyans resisted from 1911 till 1932.

The West Africans, especially those of the Muslim areas, put up the same vigorous though not so protracted or bloody a defense of their sovereignty. Thus, Lat Dior the Damel of Cayor, using both diplomatic and military means, intermittently challenged the French from about 1864 till October 1886, when in a last stand at the well of Dakhle he fell. Ba Bemba of Sikasso fought against the French from 1894 till 1898, when he heroically killed himself, preferring, as he said, death to dishonor.

The noncentralized Baule peoples in the Ivory Coast also put up a strong defense of their independence from 1891 till 1902. Behanzin and the Fon of Dahomey decided on the strategy of armed confrontation and stuck to this from 1891 until January 1894, when Behanzin was arrested, imprisoned, and then deported, first to Martinique and then to Algeria, where he died in 1906. There is no doubt that in the whole of French West Africa if not the whole of Africa, no African put up as courageous and fascinating a defense of his independence and sovereignty as Samori Ture did, as will be seen below.

Finally, in British West Africa, though the stand of the Africans was not as heroic and protracted and, as we have seen already, though many of them surrendered while others stuck to peaceful diplomacy, some nonetheless did put up a militant defense of their patrimony, especially in northern Nigeria. One of the few Yoruba states to opt for militant confrontation was Ijebu. For the purpose of teaching the Yoruba a lesson and, above all, of demonstrating to the other states of Nigeria the futility of opposition, the British launched a carefully prepared expedition of about 1,000 men, armed with the latest weapons, such as rifles, machine guns, and a maxim gun, against the Ijebu in 1892. The Ijebu raised an army of between 7,000 and 10,000 against the force, but despite their numerical superiority, they were routed. The other Yoruba states obviously learned the lesson; hence, the option of submission adopted by most of them, as has been pointed out already. In the Niger delta, Nana of the Itsikeri and, to the north of them, most of the Ibo peoples also fought the British in defense of their lands.

Even more militant and determined were the states of northern Nigeria — Nupe, Iliorin, and especially the Sokoto empire. As the sultan of Sokoto told Lugard in May 1902, "Between us and you there are no dealings except as between Musulmans and unbelievers. . . . War as God Almighty enjoined us."[37] All the rulers of the emirates refused to submit and took the field to beat back the British invaders, but they were all defeated — Kontagora in 1900, Adamawa in 1901, Bauchi in 1902, and Kano, Sokoto, and Burwuri in 1903. The sultan of Sokoto himself was deposed in 1903 and later killed. Finally in Nigeria, the Oba of Benin also bravely defended his independence until the British invaded his capital and looted its precious and fabulous art treasures (most of which are now in the British Museum) and deported him.

It should be obvious from this survey that confrontation was the most popular of the options adopted by Africans, and that all types of states and polities and all sorts of societies, regardless of size or structure, resorted to it sooner or later. Let us zoom in on two of these resistance movements — that of Samori in West Africa and then of Menelik in northeastern Africa — to see how the tactic was in fact applied.

Samori Ture's fight against not only the French but also the English in defense of the autonomy of his empire is among the most heroic episodes in the history of Africa.[38] Samori had already created a huge empire, covering the northern parts of modern Sierra Leone and Guinea and parts of Senegal, policed by a very powerful army divided into infantry and calvary wings. The infantry wing (the Sofa) by 1887 numbered between 30,000 and 35,000, and the cavalry wing was about 3,000 strong. The infantry wing was divided into permanent units of ten to twenty men known as *se*, or *Kulu*, under the command of the *Kuntigi*, and ten of these units formed a *bolo* under the command of a *bolo-kuntigi*. The cavalry wing was divided into bands of fifty each called *sere*. The *bolo* constituted the main striking force, while the *sere* moved alongside each *bolo*. Moreover, Samori's army, unlike most armies in Africa, was virtually a professional army and was armed by Samori himself. Until 1876 the army had used old guns, but from that year onwards, Samori began to arm his men with some of the most up-to-date European weapons, such as the Gras repeater rifles, which were most suitable in humid areas. From 1888 he began to add to his arms some of the new quick-firing rifles, and by 1893 he had accumulated about 6,000 of them. Not only was his army well armed, but unlike most other African armies, it was also well trained and well disciplined and had developed a sense of homogeneity. Samori financed his activities mainly from the sale of ivory as well as gold mined from the ancient gold fields of Bure (the Wangara of the Arabic writers).

The first confrontation between Samori and the French occurred in 1882 when he forced Borgnis-Desbordes, who had launched a surprise attack against him, to beat a hasty retreat. He followed this with an attack on the French on 2 April near Bamako, which he won, but he was beaten ten days later by the French. In 1885, he attacked the French who had occupied Bure, that important gold-mining area, and expelled them from that area. To strengthen his position there and to prevent the British and the French from teaming up against him, he sent emissaries to the British in Freetown and diplomatically offered to accept their protection. When the British rejected this offer, Samori, realizing the military power of the French, decided to negotiate with the latter. This resulted in a treaty in March 1886 under which he undertook to withdraw his soldiers from the right bank of the Niger

but maintained his rights over Bure. Under a revision of this treaty a year later, Samori agreed to cede the left bank of the Niger to
the French and even accepted a protectorate status. Samori, of
course, never really meant to adhere to the terms of this treaty
but merely wanted to gain the support of the French for his attack
on Tieba, the Faama of Sikasso, an attack launched in April 1887
with a 12,000-man army. The French, for their part, signed the
treaty because they wanted to prevent an alliance between
Samori and Mamadou Lamine of the Soninke, who had launched
a jihad against the French and their African protégés in January
1886 and whom they did not defeat until December 1887.

   However, when Samori saw that in spite of the treaty, the
French were assisting his rebel subjects and preventing him from
obtaining arms from Sierra Leone, he resolved on a final confrontation with them and spent two years preparing for this. He first
of all withdrew his troops from Sikasso; he then completely reorganized and retrained his army, this time along European lines;
finally, he signed a treaty with the British in Sierra Leone in May
1890 which enabled him to purchase modern weapons during the
following three years. He then launched his attack on the French
in the area of Kankan in Guinea and defeated them at the battle
of Dabadugu on 3 September 1891. The final battle of the first
phase of Samori's struggle in defense of his sovereignty occurred
in January 1892, when the French launched a well-planned invasion of the central part of Samori's empire with 1,300 carefully
picked riflemen and 3,000 porters, under the command of
Humbert. Samori personally took command of his battalion of
2,500 carefully chosen soldiers to meet Humbert, and a fierce battle ensued. Though Samori and his men fought "like demons,"[39]
they were defeated.

   After this battle, in which Samori lost about 1,000 of his best
soldiers while the French casualties numbered about 100, Samori
realized the futility of direct military confrontation with the
French. He now had two options: to surrender or to withdraw.
He of course ruled out the former and decided to withdraw eastwards to create a new empire outside the reach of the Europeans.
Adopting a scorched-earth policy, therefore, he moved eastwards towards the Bandama and Comoe rivers, encountered and

defeated a French column that was moving from the Baule country under the command of Monteil in January 1895, and occupied
Bonduku. Between July 1985 and January 1896, Samori was able
to conquer the Abron, or Gyaaman, kingdom as well as the
western part of Gonja, now part of northern Ghana. Thus, by
1896, Samori had succeeded in creating a second empire covering
the northern parts of what is now the Ivory Coast and Ghana.

From Bonduku, he dispatched envoys to Kumasi to try to form
an alliance with Prempeh and open new trade routes.[40] Prempeh
promptly and enthusiastically replied with a return mission of
300 officials and retainers that entered Bonduku in October 1895
to solicit Samori's help to "recover all the countries from Gaman
to the coast which originally belonged to Ashanti." News of this
impending alliance between Prempeh and Samori caused great
consternation and diplomatic fluttering not only in Accra but
also, and more significantly, in London. According to Wilks, it
was this consternation which precipitated the decision of the
British in 1895 to launch the massive military invasion of Asante
to forestall the French, on behalf of whom the British wrongly
thought that Samori was maneuvering.[41] This view is proved
beyond all reasonable doubt by the telegram of 15 November
1895 from Chamberlain, then British colonial secretary, to Governor Maxwell of the Gold Coast asking him to inform Samori of
the "intended action against Kumasi" and to warn him not to in-
terfere. On 20 November Maxwell did send special envoys to
deliver this message to Samori, and as we have seen already, the
British expedition entered Kumasi three months later, in January
1896, with consequences already discussed. The British then
moved troops further north under the command of Henderson;
these were defeated by Samori's forces near Wa in March 1897,
and from there Samori attacked and destroyed Kong in May
1897.

However, with the French closing in on him from the south-
west and the British from the southeast, it was obvious that
Samori's days were numbered. He was captured by the French in
a surprise attack at Guelemou on 29 September 1898 and deported to Gabon, where he died in 1900. The capture of Samori
ended what has been described as "the longest series of campaigns

against a single enemy in the history of French Sudanese conquest."[42] It is also significant that Samori resorted to all the options available — submission, alliance, diplomacy and military
confrontation — and this once again makes nonsense of the old
rigid classification of African rulers as so-called resisters and collaborators.

The second case to be looked at and this time one of success —
indeed the only success in the whole of Africa — is that of
Emperor Menelik of Ethiopia.[43] The conflict between Menelik
and the Italians really began with the Treaty of Wuchale (Italian:
Ucciali), signed between them on 2 May 1889. This treaty, which
was to signify the end of successful diplomatic relations and
launch an era of eternal friendship and cooperation, strained relations between them to such a point that only armed confrontation could resolve the impasse. Under the terms of this treaty,
Menelik recognized Italy's claim to Eritrea, including Asmara,
while Italy recognized Menelik as emperor (which was the first
such international recognition) and allowed him to import arms
through Italian territory. But the article that became so controversial was article 17 of the treaty. According to the Amharic version, Menelik could negotiate with other European powers
through Italy, but the Italian version made this obligatory. On
the basis of the latter interpretation, Italy declared Ethiopia an
Italian protectorate, and this declaration was recognized by the
other European powers. To support this claim, Italy moved
troops into northern Ethiopia and occupied Adowa in January
1890.

Menelik, of course, flatly refused to accept this interpretation.
In September 1890 he wrote to the king of Italy, Umberto I, to
point out the differences he had discovered in the two texts and
declared:

When I made that treaty of friendship with Italy, in order that our
secrets be guarded and that our understanding should not be spoiled, I
said that because of our friendship our affairs in Europe might be carried on with the aid of the Sovereign of Italy, but I have not made any
treaty which obliges me to do so, and today, I am not the man to accept
it. That one independent power does not seek the aid of another to
carry on its affairs your Majesty understands very well.[44]

The Italians, however, would not budge. Instead, they declared that "Italy cannot notify the other powers that she was mistaken in Article XVII, because she must maintain her dignity." To this statement, Menelik's consort, Empress Taytu, retorted: "We also have made known to the Powers that the said Article, as it is written in our language, has another meaning. As you, we also ought to respect our dignity. You wish Ethiopia to be represented before the other Powers as your protectorate, but this shall never be."[45] After importing large quantities of firearms, mainly from France and Russia (by 1893 Ethiopia had acquired 82,000 rifles and 28 canons), Menelik formally and finally repudiated the Wuchale treaty on 12 February 1893. Two weeks later, he announced this repudiation to the other European powers. In this announcement he referred to Italy's claims and made the famous declaration: "Ethiopia has need of no one; she stretches her hand unto God."

The virtually inevitable clash began in January 1895, when the Italians attacked and occupied Tigre. Menelik replied by issuing his famous mobilization order on 17 September and marched north with a huge army which defeated the Italians at Amba Alagi and Magale in December. The Italians then retreated to Adowa, where the final battle in January 1896 resulted in the total defeat and rioting of the Italian army. The Italian casualties consisted of 261 officers, 2,918 noncommissioned officers and men, and about 2,000 *askaris*, or local troops, killed; 954 Italian soldiers missing; and 470 Italians and 958 askaris wounded — in sum, over 40 percent of the fighting force of the Italians.

This Ethiopian victory — described by Akpan as "the greatest victory of an African over a European army since the time of Hannibal"[46] and the only decisive victory won by an African country throughout the whole period of the Partition and occupation — was of very great significance. First, it ensured the continued sovereignty of Ethiopia. Following that victory the Italians signed the Peace Treaty of Addis Ababa on 26 October 1896; this treaty abrogated the Wuchale treaty and recognized the total independence of Ethiopia, an independence also recognized by the other European powers. Secondly, the victory spread the fame of Ethiopia throughout the world. Above all, the victory filled the hearts of blacks throughout the world with racial pride, and the name of Ethiopia became their symbol of hope, survival, and regeneration.

Thus, the Africans did not readily surrender their sovereignty but, rather, resorted to all possible measures to defend it. In the end, all of them failed except Ethiopia and Liberia. The final question to be answered, then, is why these two countries succeeded while all the others failed. In the case of Ethiopia, the answer has already been given — namely, the decisive victory at Adowa, achieved primarily because, for the first time in all the Afro-European military encounters, the African side enjoyed the technological and military superiority. At the battle of Adowa, the Ethiopian army was over 100,000 strong, while the Italian army consisted of only about 17,000 men, of whom 10,596 were Italians and the rest Eritrean levies. But what was even more decisive was that the Ethiopian army, unlike most African armies, was armed with modern rifles and even canons. The combination of these two factors explains Ethiopia's historic victory. Liberia, on the other hand, survived partly because of her diplomatic skill in playing one imperial power against another, partly because of the support she enjoyed from the United States, which was not prepared to see her gobbled up, and mainly because neither Germany nor France nor Britain was prepared to see Liberia acquired by anyone of them.

From the above, some of the reasons for the failure of the rest of the African states to maintain their sovereignty should be obvious. There is no doubt that the most crucial of these reasons was military. First, most of these African armies were nonprofessional and not properly trained. Secondly, contrary to popular opinion, the African armies were, as recent research has clearly demonstrated, in many cases numerically inferior to the European armies. It should not be forgotten that most of the armies of the European imperialists consisted of African soldiers and thousands of African auxiliaries, usually recruited from annexed or protected or allied territories, and it was only the officer corps that was usually European. And it is quite clear from the Ethiopian case that numerical superiority did count. Above all, technologically and logistically, African armies were at a great disadvantage in comparison with their invaders. None of them ever had any logistic support of any kind, and an overwhelming majority of them were armed with completely outmoded guns, little artillery, and such traditional weapons as spears, javelins, cudgels, bows and arrows, and even charms and amulets. Nor did any of them have a navy. What chance would such an army have against a well-trained, professional one armed with cannons and repeater rifles like the maxim guns and enjoying naval and logistic support? That the Ethiopian army, equipped with the latest weapons and enjoying numerical superiority, succeeded and survived proves beyond any doubt the crucial importance of this military factor.

There were, however, other factors which were important though not so crucial. First, no African state was strong enough economically to have sustained any protracted warfare against any of the imperial powers. In most cases, therefore, the defeat of any one of them was only a matter of time. Secondly, though some African rulers and leaders felt the need for alliances and, indeed, formed a few of them — the Lunda and the Chokwe allied against the Congo State army, while the Barue succeeded in bringing the Tonga, Tawara, and a number of Shona peoples together against the British in Southern Rhodesia — most African rulers failed to form any such alliances. Not only did this failure weaken them militarily, but it also enabled the European imperialists to play one African power against the other. Had Samori, Ahmadu, Lat Dior, and Mamadou Lamine, or even the first two alone, allied against the French, the course of events in the Senegambia region could well have been different. But they never did, and they thereby allowed the French not only to play one against the other but to defeat each one in isolation. It was for all these reasons, and above all, as Hilaire Belloc declared, because the Europeans had the maxim gun and the Africans did not, that an overwhelming number of African states lost their independence.

CHAPTER THREE

The Operation of the Colonial System

B y the end of the first decade of this century, despite the spirited defense and opposition put up by the Africans, the colonial imperialist conquest and occupation had been almost completed, thanks mainly to the maxim gun; and the continent of Africa had been carved up into colonies of different sizes and shapes among the imperial powers of Britain, France, Germany, Italy, Spain, and Portugal. As we have seen, the most important reasons for the partition and occupation of Africa were the need for raw materials to feed the factories of industrial Europe and the need for markets for the sale of manufactured goods. To attain these two main ends, a number of prerequisites would have to be met: peace and order would have to be established and maintained; the primary means of production in the form of land, labor, and capital would have to be guaranteed; an infrastructure of roads, railways, telegraphs, and telephones would have to be provided; medical facilities would have to be provided to ensure the health of the European administrators, traders, farmers, miners, and in some cases settlers; finally, some education would have to be provided to produce educated Africans to be employed in the various sectors of the economy as well as in the civil service. What, then, were the measures that were introduced to provide these necessary prerequisites? How did these various measures work and with what success? Finally, what were the African initiatives and responses in the light of all these colonial activities? Since the first two questions are the usual questions that are dealt with in most of the existing works on colonialism,[1] I will touch on them only very briefly here and concentrate on the third.

To provide the above prerequisites, all the colonial imperial powers first and foremost set up systems of administration, either for each individual colony, as the British and the Germans did, or for a group of colonies, as the French did. Each colony was placed under a governor. In many cases, he was to administer the colony with the assistance of a council of advisors or a legislative and executive council. For the purpose of local and regional administration, each colony was divided into regions under regional commissioners and districts under district commissioners. At the local level, some of the imperial powers made use of existing traditional rulers. The British certainly did so, and even where none existed created them under their so-called system of indirect rule. The French, on the other hand, abolished most of the traditional ruling dynasties or, like the Belgians, drastically reduced their number and instead appointed educated Africans as chiefs to control local areas. Courts were also set up in all the colonies to administer justice, usually in accordance with metropolitan laws. Police forces and armies — such as the Force Publique of the Congo, the Guerras Pretas of Angola, the Sepais of Mozambique, and the British Native Police of Northern Rhodesia — were created, and colonial armies were constituted or maintained, all to ensure order, peace, and security.

In the social field, hospitals were built, though they were found mainly in the urban centers to serve the expatriate communities. Other amenities such as piped water, electricity, dispensaries, paved streets, and the like were also provided, but again mainly for the urban centers. Some educational facilities were established at the elementary level and in few cases at the secondary level, either through missionary-society grants or through colonial government funding. It was partly to finance these administrative and social services and partly to ensure a regular supply of labor that both direct and indirect taxation was introduced.

To safeguard the interests of the expatriate communities and in conformity with the racist ideas of the day, discrimination was practiced in one form or another by all the colonial powers —

more crude and overt in the French colonies and more subtle and covert in the British and Germany colonies. To varying degrees all the colonial rulers also condemned everything African in the cultural field and tried to produce Africans in their own image. The French and the Portuguese even conferred certain citizenship and legal rights on those who managed to pass this acculturation test; these Africans became known as *evolvués* and *assimilados* or *nâos indigenas*, respectively.

It was in the economic field, of course, that the colonial powers exerted their greatest efforts.[2] In each colony, an infrastructure of roads, railways, and harbors was provided, obviously to facilitate the movement not only of raw materials and manufactured goods and heavy machinery, especially for the mining industry, but also of troops and policemen. Indeed, by the end of the Second World War, the infrastructure of most African states as are known even today had been completed. Every encouragement was given to expatriate companies and individuals to set up farms and plantations and enter the mining field. All the colonial administrators also ensured that land was made available to Europeans, mainly through confiscation and the expulsion and resettlement of the indigenous peoples. In all such areas, compulsory labor was practiced on a very large scale, especially in the early decades of the system, while migrant labor was also provided and the pass system was introduced to ensure the availability of labor. In those colonies which for environmental reasons were unsuitable for the settlement of Europeans, the indigenous Africans were assisted to produce the raw materials so urgently needed.

In some colonies, especially in the Belgian and Portuguese colonies, Africans were in fact forced to grow certain cash crops, such as cotton, and set production targets, say for rubber — especially in the Belgian Congo — and those who failed to reach those targets were treated with extreme brutality.[3] In most cases, Africans were made to concentrate on a single cash crop or two in each colony, and with some success. Since so much attention was focused on the production of cash crops, that of foodstuffs was neglected, and food therefore had to be imported.

Furthermore, expatriate firms and companies were given every

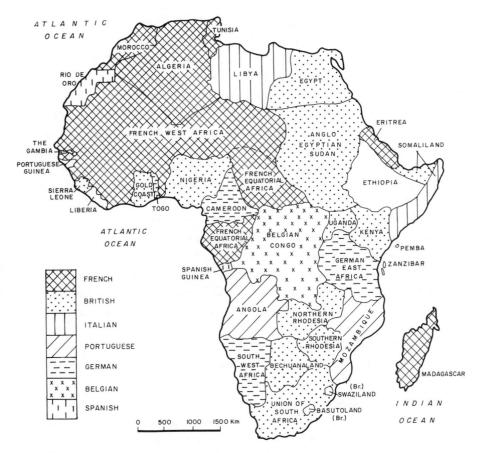

AFRICA UNDER COLONIAL RULE

opportunity to import manufactured goods, usually from the metropolitan countries, and to export the raw materials – sisal, minerals, cotton, peanuts, cocoa, cloves – being produced, and the pricing of both the imports and the exports was left exclusively in the hands of those companies. The main consequence of this policy was the elimination of Africans from the import-export business. To finance these economic activities expatriate-owned banks were allowed to operate in these colonies; all of these banks discriminated against African entrepreneurs in their granting of loans. Africans were also banned from the lucrative mining enterprises, which became the exclusive preserve of European companies and oligopolies. Finally, the political economy of colonialism was characterized by the virtually total neglect of industrialization and manufacturing and the refusal to process locally produced raw materials.

Such, in short, was the nature of the colonial system. Its main *raison d'être* was the ruthless exploitation of the human and material resources of the African continent to the advantage of the owners and shareholders of expatriate companies and the metropolitan governments and their manufacturing and industrial firms. What, then, were the reactions and responses of the Africans to all this?

Many European historians are of the opinion that all classes and groups of Africans with the sole exception of the educated elite readily accepted colonial rule and that it was not until the return home of those who had been educated abroad, especially in the United States and the United Kingdom, that the reaction against colonialism was set in motion. According to such scholars, then, the attack on the colonial system was the concern of the educated elite only, and it did not begin until either the interwar period or after the Second World War. One of them, Margery Perham, writes:

Most of the tribes quickly accepted European rule as part of an irresistible order, one which brought many benefits, above all, peace, and exciting novelties, railways and roads, lamps, bicycles, ploughs. . . . For the ruling classes, traditional or created, it brought a new strength and security of status and new forms of wealth and power. . . . It was not until a small minority, through their attainment of the higher levels of Western education, and above all through travel came to understand something of the world at large and of their own place in it that the spell of acceptance began to be broken. Excited by the wine of these ideas, and smarting, perhaps, from some experience of the colour bar in Europe, and especially in Britain, the young African would return after some years to his country to preach the idea that only by self-government could Africans escape from personal humiliation and win equality of status in a world of which they were at last becoming aware.[4]

These views are clearly the products of the old colonial, or Eurocentric, African historiography, which seeks to explain most events and developments in Africa in external terms, and in this case, in terms of the frustration of the foreign-educated elite. But these views are totally erroneous. It was not *after* the Second World War that Africans became conscious of the iniquities, inhumanity, oppression, and exploitation of the colonial system and then began to react to it, but within a few years of its establishment. Secondly, this awareness or nationalist feeling was not confined to the educated elite but extended to all classes and groups of Africans, the traditional as well as the educated elite, illiterate farmers and traders, merchant princes, and civil servants, rural as well as urban dwellers.

To analyze these anticolonial or nationalist reactions effectively, I shall divide the colonial era into three main periods. These are the periods roughly from the 1890s to about the end of the First World War, then from 1919 to 1935, and finally from 1935 to the 1960s. This periodization, far from being arbitrary, is very much determined by the objectives being pursued by the Africans, by the nature of the leadership provided, and, above all, by the strategies that were resorted to. I have chosen 1935 as the final year of the second period rather than the more usual 1939 because the latter, which signifies the beginning of the Second World War, is an Eurocentric one and is not of as much real significance for Africa as 1935, which marks the Fascist Italian occupation of Ethiopia. Only the first two periods will be dealt with here.

During the first period, the illiterate and traditional rulers of the rural areas and the educated elite and the urban dwellers reacted differently in terms of objectives, leadership, and strategies. In the rural areas, the most widespread strategy was rebellion and insurrection, either localized or widespread, with the objective in most cases of overthrowing the recently imposed colonial system. Most of these revolts were led, as in the earlier defensive wars, by the traditional rulers and were precipitated by some of the colonial measures that have been mentioned above — either taxation, land alienation, compulsory cultivation of crops, the tyrannical behavior of colonial officials, or the introduction of Western education and with it the condemnation of African culture and traditional ways of life. Typical examples of these rebellions in West Africa are the Hut Tax Rebellion that broke out in Sierra Leone in 1898; the rebellion of 1900 in Asante in Ghana against direct taxation, compulsory labor, and the introduction of Western education and finally the demand for the Golden Stool, which was led by the famous Asante queen Yaa Asantewa; the Ekumeku rebellion in Nigeria, which lasted from 1893 till 1906, in defense of the old order; the Egba revolt, or the Adube War, of 1918 against direct taxation and forced labor; the rising between 1898 and 1902 in eastern Nigeria; the rebellions of the Mossi in Kouddigou and Fada N'gourma from 1908 to 1914, of the Gurunsi in 1915–16 in Upper Volta (now Burkina Faso), and of the Lobi and Dyula in Mali between 1908 and 1909; and the numerous uprisings in several parts of Guinea and the Ivory Coast between 1908 and 1914.

In southern Africa, these insurrections included the Ndebele-Shona *chimurenga* (rebellion) of 1896–97, the Bambala or Zulu rebellion of 1906, and the Herero revolt of 1904. In Central Africa, there were the Manjanga insurrection in the Lower Congo against labor recruitment and the numerous uprisings in the Zambesi Valley between 1890 and 1905 — at least sixteen of them have been counted — mainly against the hut tax and forced labor. According to Isaacman and Vansina, from 1885 to 1918 more than twenty insurrections that were mass uprisings cutting across ethnic boundaries occurred in the five central African colonies of Angola, Mozambique, Nyasaland, Northern Rhodesia, and the Congo with the aim of expelling the colonialists. A majority of them occurred in the Portuguese colonies and the Congo, "where the combination of extremely oppressive rule and a weak administrative and military structure precipitated recurring revolutionary activity."[5]

Cult priests and spirit mediums of traditional African religion were involved in or led some of these insurrections. For instance, the Tonga priest Maluma of Nyasaland told his people in 1909 that "the time has come for us to fight the white people, we will start now and fight through the rainy season. The black people [will] rise and drive all the white people out of the country." He went on to lead the Tonga in a rebellion against the British.[6] Similarly, the Mbona cult priest led the Massingire rebellion of

1884, while in the Congo, the cult priestess Maria Nkoie provided her followers with charms which were supposed to render them immune to European guns and led them in a revolt which lasted from 1916 till 1921. Shona spirit mediums were also definitely behind the unsuccessful rebellions of 1897, 1901, and 1904 in the Zambesi Valley.

In East Africa, there was the rebellion of 1913 inspired by the Mumbo cult and led by its founder, Onyango Dande, aimed at overthrowing the oppressive colonial system in Kenya. The Akamba of eastern Kenya, inspired first by the female priestess Siofume, and then by a young man, Kiamba, rose against the British in 1911. The Giriama of Kenya also revolted against colonial rule in 1914 during the war. In Uganda, the Acholi revolted in 1911 against labor recruitment.

The most famous rebellion in East Africa, however, was the Maji Maji rebellion, which aimed at expelling the Germans from Tanganyika. It broke out in 1905 under the leadership of the traditional prophet Kinjikitile Ngwale. This rebellion spread over an area of more than 10,000 square miles and involved over twenty different ethnic groups. It was primarily against forced labor, taxation, and oppression and was precipitated by the introduction of a new communal cotton scheme under which people were to work on the cotton farms for twenty-eight days a year. Unlike most of the other revolts, this was a real mass movement of peasants and, in the words of Iliffe, was "the final attempt by Tanganyika's old societies to destroy the colonial order by force."[7]

In Madagascar there occurred the famous widespread rebellions of 1904–5, which, according to Jacob, were "a fight for independence and a struggle against colonial exploitation";[8] in addition, the Sadiavahe, an armed peasant uprising, broke out in 1915 in the southwestern part of the island, precipitated partly by the imposition of a cattle tax and partly by the compulsory recruitment of soldiers for the First World War. In the Sudan, there were many Mahdist uprisings against the colonial system in 1900, 1902–3, and 1904. In Somaliland a rebellion led by al-Sayyid Muhammad for the overthrow of the colonial system raged from 1895 till the leader's death in 1920. Particularly numerous were the revolts and insurrections in many parts of Africa during the First World War, especially in British, French, and German colonies.

All these rebellions and insurrections were brutally suppressed, with thousands of Africans killed. The suppression of the Egba revolt of 1918 in Nigeria, for instance, was accomplished by one of the largest military operations to be mounted by the British in West Africa, involving a total of 2,500 African troops and 70 Europeans and resulting in the destruction of about twenty Egba towns. According to A. J. Temu, the suppression of the Maji Maji rebellion in Tanganyika left 75,000 dead, while the uprising in South-West Africa led to a loss of about half the entire population of the colony.[9]

Although rebellions and insurrections were the most popular and widespread forms of African resistance, they were not the only strategies used by the rural folk and their leaders in their struggle against colonial domination and exploitation. Another strategy often adopted was migration or flight across international boundaries.[10] This strategy was particularly popular among the Africans in the French, Belgian, German, and Portuguese colonies, mainly because of rampant forced labor, oppressive direct taxation, compulsory cultivation of crops, and, in the case of the French colonies, the *indigenat* — that is, the arbitrary and rough-and-ready way of administering justice and the use of corporal punishment. Thus, in 1916 and 1917, more than 2,000 people left the Ivory Coast for Ghana. Large numbers also left Togo for Ghana during the period, and in 1910 alone as many as 14,000 migrated from the district of Misahohe into Ghana.

Those who lived near or along international borders, such as the Angola-Congo border or the Nyasaland-Mozambique border, slipped across them to avoid tax collectors. According to some official sources, 50,000 Africans living in the Zambesi Valley escaped into Southern Rhodesia and Nyasaland between 1895 and 1907. The Ovambo and the Bakongo from Angola, and the Shona and Chewa from Mozambique, slipped across the borders to Nyasaland to join their kinsmen there. As Isaacman and Vansina have shown, some of these groups, rather than crossing the border, withdrew into the inaccessible parts of the colony and created refugee communities. In their new areas, out of reach of the colonial rulers, they "attained a kind of independence which they fiercely and jealously guarded," rather like the Maroon communities of the Americas.[11] This practice was widespread in the Gambo region of southern Angola, and in the forest and mountainous areas of the Congo.

Some of these refugee communities under their leaders not only guarded their independence, but also resorted to attacking what they considered to be the symbols of colonial oppression and exploitation: plantations, warehouses, shops of rural merchants, tax collectors, labor recruiters, and so on. These people were often successful because they enjoyed the support of the rural population, from whom they received such things as food, ammunition, and useful strategic information. The most famous of these leaders was Mapondera, who successfully harassed the British and Portuguese forces in Southern Rhodesia from 1892 till 1903. Isaacman and Vansina have categorized these leaders as social bandits and their activities as social banditry.[12] Because of the rather unpleasant connotations of these terms, I find them unacceptable and prefer the terms *commando leaders* and *commando activities*.

Besides rebellions and migrations, the rural and illiterate people resorted to such passive resistance as refusal to comply with orders, absenteeism, feigned illness, loafing and work slowdowns, refusal to cultivate compulsory crops, and above all, rejecting all the "civilized" innovations introduced by or connected with the colonial system or the foreign presence, whether schools, churches, or the colonial languages. Thus, the people of Togo in the German area refused to send their children to the German schools or learn the German language in preference to the English schools and language.

Unlike the rural people and the traditionalists, the educated elite and the workers in the urban and mining centers, rather than aiming at the overthrow of the colonial system, generally worked for its reform during this period. Their main objectives were the correction of certain abuses; the provision of facilities, especially in the educational and economic fields; and adequate representation on the legislative and executive councils. The channels that they created for the articulation of these objectives as well as grievances were a host of open and secret societies, associations, unions, political parties, and new African-controlled Ethiopian and millenarian or Pentecostal churches. The means they used to attain their objectives were literary media such as the press, plays, pamphlets, novels, and poetry; petitions and delegations to the legislative councils and metropolitan governments; and, to a very limited extent, strikes and boycotts. Though the leadership here was by and large confined to the educated elite, there were some instances in which it was shared with the traditional elite.

One of the instruments that became increasingly important for the expression of the demands and criticisms of the educated elite was the press. Indeed, during this period, there was a mushrooming of newspapers in the coastal urban centers. Between 1890 and 1919 about ten newspapers were founded in Ghana alone, either in Accra or in Cape Coast, among which were the *Gold Coast Aborigines* (1898), the *Gold Coast Free Press* (1899), and the *Gold Coast Leader* (1902).[13] Five were founded in Nigeria: the *Lagos Standard* (1895), the *Lagos Weekly Record* (1891), the *Nigerian Chronicle* (1908), the *Nigerian Pioneer* (1914), and the *Nigerian Times* (1910). In South Africa as early as 1884 J. T. Jabavu founded the first African newspaper, *Imvozaba Ntsundu* (Native Opinion), printed in both English and Xhosa; and by 1915, there were five major newspapers there. In Uganda the *Ebifa Mu Uganda* was founded in 1907. (None was founded in Kenya or Tanzania until after the period under review.) All these newspapers were full of attacks on the colonial system.

A number of societies, associations, and political parties were formed during this period to lead the campaign against the colonial system. Among those founded in West Africa were the Fantsi Amanbuhu Fekuw (the Fante National Political and Cultural Society) and the Aborigines' Rights Protection Society (ARPS), both founded in Cape Coast in Ghana in 1888 and 1897, respectively; the Young Senegalese Club in 1910; and the People's Union and the Anti-Slavery and Aborigines Society formed in Nigeria by the educated elite and the traditional rulers in 1908 and 1912, respectively. The Fantsi Amambuhu Fekuw, which was derisively called "Gone Fantee" by the Europeans on the coast, was formed in response to the sudden awareness among the Cape Coast educated elite of the harmful and demoralizing nature of the European impact on their culture. Its main aim, therefore, was "to stop further encroachments into their nationality." As Mensah Sarbah, one of the moving spirits and the leading cultural nationalist of the day later explained in terms which merit quotation,

Fully convinced that it is better to be called by one's own name than to be known by a foreign one, that it is possible to acquire Western learning and be expert in scientific attainments without neglecting one's mother-tongue, that the African's dress had a closer resemblance to the garb of the Grecian and Roman . . . and should not be thrown aside, even if one wears European dress during business hours – Japan having since shown it is possible to retain one's national costume and yet excel in wisdom and knowledge – I say, Gold Coast men, by means of the "Mfantsi Amanbuhu Fekuw," . . . impressed upon the people the necessity to reconsider the future of their native land.[14]

In 1897 this cultural society was converted into the Aborigines' Rights Protection Society, which soon became one of the most interesting societies to be formed in West Africa during the period under review.[15] Its immediate aim was to protest against the Land Bill proposed by the British colonial government. This bill, which was to convert all so-called empty lands into government lands, caused great alarm and raised a storm of protest and uproar throughout the country. The other aims of the ARPS were to discuss "the various bills intended to be passed by the Government from time to time with a view of fully understanding the meaning, purport, object and effect thereof," and to press for constitutional reforms, the abolition of direct taxation, and better and higher education. As the society's mouthpiece, the *Gold Coast Aborigines*, put it in 1902, "We want educated Fantis not Europeanized natives. We simply want our education to enable us to develop and to improve our native ideas, customs, manners and institutions." Indeed, for this purpose, the society established some elementary schools and one secondary school in Cape Coast in 1905, the Mfantsipim School, with the Akan motto "Dwen Hwe Kan" ("Think and Look Ahead"), rather than the usual Latin motto. In other words, the society was formed to serve as the watchdog and mouthpiece of the interests of the people and a critic of the colonial system.

What makes this society even more interesting are the methods that it applied to achieve its aims. The first was a press campaign; as indicated above, the society founded its own newspaper, the *Gold Coast Aborigines*. The second was direct appeals to the Legislative Council. Thus, in June 1897, the ARPS asked for and was granted permission to send two representatives to the Legislative Council to plead its case, and this was done from the bar of the House by two lawyers, Mensah Sarbah and Awooner Renner. The third weapon was the dispatch of delegations to Europe. In May 1898 the ARPS sent a deputation to England to state "the grounds of the public objections to the Land Bill." The cost of this delegation was met out of funds contributed mainly by the traditional rulers. As a result of its agitation in England, both the Land Bill and the Hut Tax or Poll Tax then being introduced were dropped, though its demand for constitutional reforms was rejected.

The People's Union of Lagos was also formed to protest against the land law, the taxation policy, and the attempts being made by the colonial government to control the press. Like the ARPS it also sent a delegation to London besides the usual press campaign.

In French West Africa, the Young Senegalese Club also campaigned for jobs, better and equal salaries, abolition of discrimination in education, and racial equality. Another party that was active in the Senegal during this period was the Republican Socialist Party, founded by Blaise Diagne. With its help, as well as the support of the Muslim leaders and the Young Senegalese Club, Diagne won the elections of 1914 and became the first black African deputy to the French Parliament.[16]

A movement comparable to the ARPS was the South African Native National Congress, formed in South Africa in 1912. The moving spirits behind this were Pixley Ka Izaka Seme, who had just returned from his studies in the United States, and Solomon Plaatje, described as "a highly cultured Tswana journalist and writer." The main aim of the Congress was to champion the cause of Africans, especially in view of the formation of the Union of

South Africa in 1910. One of its first acts was to protest against the Natives Land Act of 1913, which made it illegal for Africans to acquire land outside their own areas. The Congress continued to meet annually, and it spearheaded nationalist activities until, as will be seen later, it was momentarily eclipsed by the Industrial and Commercial Union, founded in 1919 by Clements Kadalie.

In central Africa, similar anticolonial associations and societies were founded. In 1912, the North Nyasa Native Association was founded in Nyasaland, and two years later the West Nyasa Native Association emerged. Among the demands of these associations were increased educational facilities, higher pay and better conditions of service for workers, increased economic activities, and reform of the forced labor system and taxation. In Angola in 1906, the mulatto intellectuals also formed their first association to press for their rights, using the newspapers as their main medium. In 1910, a union of all mulatto intellectuals throughout the Portuguese colonies was established. The Liga Angolana, an association of Angolan civil servants, was also formed and gained official recognition in 1913.

In Madagascar the secret society known as VVS (Vy Vato Sakelike, meaning "strong and hard like stone and iron") was established in 1913 by seven medical students who had been inspired by the series of articles written by the Protestant minister Ravelojaona under the title "Japan and the Japanese."[17] In these articles, Ravelojaona, rather like Mensah Sarbah of Ghana, had appealed to the Malagasy to follow the Japanese model by not repudiating their culture and tradition but rather by blending them with modernism. The VVS — which soon attracted clerks, office workers, and primary school teachers — used the press to call on the Malagasy to "sacrifice themselves for their homeland so that its people could advance and live in freedom and dignity." This secret society was, however, tracked down by the French, who suppressed it with extreme brutality. It was not until after the First World War that anticolonial or nationalist activities were resumed in Madagascar.

In Egypt, similar associations and parties were formed; these included Hizb al-Islah al-Dusturi (the Constitutional Reformers), founded by the famous Pan-Islamist writer Sheikh Ali Yusuf in

1907, and the Nationalist Party, founded officially in the same year by the charismatic leader, scholar, and orator Mustafa Kamil.[18] Unlike the other societies and parties, these Egyptian societies demanded the evacuation of the British from Egypt and complete autonomy. It was to promote these causes that Kamil toured Europe between 1895 and 1898. Following the premature death of Kamil in February 1908 and the imprisonment of his successor, Muhammad Farid, by the British in 1911 and his voluntary exile after his release, the radical nationalist movement disintegrated.

Though trade union activities were not allowed during this period, there were nevertheless strikes and boycotts, usually by urban workers to obtain higher wages or reduced prices of imported goods or in protest against ill treatment of workers. Thus, there was a strike by the workers on the Dakar–St. Louis line in 1890. In 1891, the women of Dahomey employed in the Cameroons went on strike. Workers in Lagos went on strike for higher pay in 1897. According to Basil Davidson, this was "the first major colonial strike."[19] In 1918–19 there was a strike by the Cotonou and Grand Popo paddlers in Dahomey. In Mozambique, employees of the Merchants' Association struck in 1913, train workers in 1917, and railroad technicians in 1918. In South Africa, there were strikes by sewage and garbage collectors in Johannesburg in 1917 and by Transvaal miners in 1918. That same year saw the first mass boycott of goods staged by the miners in eastern Witwatersrand. On 1 July 1918, Africans working in three mines in the Cape Colony went on strike. In East Africa, the first known strike in Kenya, that by African police constables, occurred in Mombasa in 1902; in 1908 African railway workers struck at Mazeras, followed by African rickshaw pullers in the same year, and in 1916, by the boatmen in Mombasa. Nevertheless, strikes were not much used as a weapon during this period, and as is obvious from this brief catalogue, they were resorted to only toward the end of the period.

Besides associations and parties, the other channels used by the educated elite in their anticolonial campaigns were independent Christian churches. These were of two categories: the Ethiopian churches, which emphasized African self-improvement, self-rule, and political rights; and the millenarian or pentecostal churches, which derived their inspiration from their apocalyptic vision of divine intervention and emphasized possession by the Holy Spirit, healing, and prophesy. The emergence of these churches in Africa coincided with the beginnings of the establishment of the colonial system.

These Ethiopian and millenarian church movements were particularly strong in South Africa and Malawi. As we have seen already, the first of these churches, the Tembu Church, was founded in South Africa in 1884 by Nehemiah Tile. According to Sundkler, a European missionary's criticism of the founder because of "his strong Tembu nationalistic sympathies" caused Tile to leave the Wesleyan Mission Church and found his own church two years later.[20] The second one, which was also the first to be called Ethiopian — the South African Ethiopian Church — was founded in central Africa by Willie J. Mokalapa in 1892. Among the passages from which the founder claimed to have derived inspiration was Psalm 68:31 — "Ethiopia shall soon stretch out her hands unto God" — and he talked about "the self-government of the African Church under African leaders." The first of these churches to be established in West Africa was the Native Baptist Church, founded in Nigeria in 1888 by a group of Nigerian leaders of the Southern Baptist Mission; the second was founded by some Yoruba Methodists in 1891. The latter stated their reason for their move in clear terms: "That this meeting, in humble dependence upon Almighty God, is of the opinion that Africa is to be evangelized, and that foreign agencies at work at the present moment, taking into consideration climatic and other influences, cannot grasp the situation. . . . That a purely Native Church can be founded for the evangelization and amelioration of our race, to be governed by Africans."[21]

In 1909 Kamwana founded the first Watchtower, or Apostolic, Church in Nyasaland. The formation of this church, as well as others in southern Africa, was definitely influenced by the Christian Catholic Apostolic Church of Zion, Illinois, whose missionaries arrived in southern Africa in 1904. Their activities led to the formation not only of this church but the emergence of a whole series of churches known as Zion, Jerusalem, Apostolic,

Full Gospel, Pentecostal, and so on, in that area. Kamwana demanded free education and books; he also attacked the levying of taxes. Indeed, he went out of his way to prophesy that in 1914 British rule would come to an end. He told his people, "We shall build our own ships, make our own powder and make or import our own guns."[22] He was, of course, soon arrested and exiled, which only accelerated the spread of his movement to many parts of Nyasaland.

Even more interesting was the church founded by Charles Domingo, again in Nyasaland, in 1911 among the northern Nguni. In his sermons, he attacked the Christian missions and the Europeans, pointing out the contrast between their theories and practices. In 1910, John Owalo also founded the first really independent church in Kenya, the Nomiya Luo Church.

As we shall see below, these churches became more numerous during the 1920s and 1930s. But it should be evident from the above and especially from their objectives that these Ethiopian and pentecostal churches were as anticolonial as they were antimissionary, and it is this that justifies the view of Oliver and Atmore that the Christian-educated Africans were the first African nationalists.[23]

It would appear that only one educated African resorted to rebellion during this period, and that was Rev. John Chilembwe of Malawi.[24] Chilembwe went to the United States in the company of the radical European evangelist, John Booth in 1897 and returned three years later to his hometown, Chiradzulu, as an ordained minister. Here he established the Providence Industrial Mission, which ran schools and farms. For ten years, he tried to work within the colonial framework. However, the economic difficulties being faced by the people, intensified by the famine of 1913 and, above all, the conscription of carriers and men for the war, turned him into an anti-European leader, and in his sermons he attacked colonialism as a mockery of Christianity. In 1914, he condemned African participation in the war. "Let the rich men, bankers, titled men, storekeepers, farmers and landlords go to war and get shot," he wrote to a local newspaper in November 1914; "instead, the poor Africans who have nothing to own in this present world, who in death leave only a long line of widows and orphans in utter want and dire distress, are invited to die for a cause which is not theirs." In January 1915 he raised the standard of revolt, but the rebellion was suppressed and Chilembwe himself was shot during the course of it.

Thus, between the 1880s and the 1910s Africans, both literate and illiterate, both urban and rural, both kings and subjects, and laymen as well as priests, applied all sorts of strategies either to overthrow or more popularly still to reform the colonial system. These anticolonial or nationalist activities did achieve some successes. In some areas, direct taxation and the seizure of lands were stopped, at least by the British, while the Germans certainly introduced some useful reforms after the Maji Maji rebellion. Though demands for constitutional reforms were rejected in the British areas, some concessions were made at least in the four communes of Senegal. But these successes were exceedingly limited and did not make any dent whatsoever on the colonial system itself. The reason for this failure was primarily because the colonial powers were in no mood for any real reform of the system, while they were only too ready to resort to the most violent and brutal of measures to suppress any protest movement, be it peaceful or violent, moderate or radical, during the period under review.

In the period between the end of the First World War and the Fascist occupation of Ethiopia in 1935 African initiatives and reactions in the face of the oppressive and exploitative colonial system continued. While there were some differences between African reactions in the two periods, these differences were, with a few notable exceptions, more of degree than of kind, of an intensification and a more sophisticated application of the old strategies than a refashioning of completely new ones, and more of the involvement of a greater number of people. As in the previous period, only a relatively small number of the African nationalists and agitators demanded a complete overthrow of the colonial system. Moreover, with the exception of Wallace Johnson's Youth League in West Africa and a few branches of Garvey's Universal Negro Improvement Association (UNIA) in West Africa and elsewhere in Africa,[25] to be discussed below, all such radical demands were confined to the states of northern

Africa, where reactions were exacerbated by the dialectic between religion and nationalism. It was in the area of leadership
that one notices a fundamental change between the first and second periods. Whereas in most parts of Africa, in both the rural
and urban areas, traditional rulers played some role during the
former period, in the latter period — with the significant exception of North Africa — the educated elite in the urban areas and
the young workers and peasants in the rural areas took over the
leadership. Indeed, during this period, the anticolonial campaign
became a tripartite affair involving the educated elite, the colonial authorities, and the traditional rulers.

The fundamental difference in scale between the initiatives and
reactions in the two periods can be attributed to a number of
factors — the changing nature of the colonial system itself during
the second period, the economic depression that characterized
the period, the impact of the First World War, and finally the impact of the Pan-Africanist and communist activities of the period.
Let us look at each of these factors briefly before examining the
initiatives and responses themselves.

The period 1919–35 was colonial imperialism's last territorial
drive in Africa. By 1935, all those areas that were still holding out
against the imperialists and clinging to their sovereignty — the Rif
areas in northwest Africa, the eastern parts of Kenya, the Darfur
area in the Sudan, the Lunda homelands of Quico in Angola, the
Makonde highlands of Mozambique, and the Obbia districts in
Somaliland — were all brought under effective occupation and
put under the colonial system. This meant that more Africans
were feeling the pinch of colonialism by the 1920s than were by
the 1910s. One would therefore expect to see a corresponding
change in the scale of anticolonialist or nationalist activities.
Moreover, the new administrative measures and ordinances that
were introduced during this period to underpin the colonial
system — this was the heyday of the British system of "indirect
rule" — gave more and more powers to the traditional rulers and
the newly created chiefs to the exclusion of the educated elite.
Frustration and disappointment therefore grew among the
educated elite, and since their number increased during the
period, their reactions became not only intensified and anti-

colonial but anti–traditional rulers as well. Finally, the process of urbanization gathered momentum during the period as more and more people drifted into the towns for employment while the number of workers, especially in the mines and on the plantations, increased, especially in South and Central Africa. It is estimated that by 1935 more than 900,000 peasants were involved in the compulsory production of cotton in the Belgian Congo alone. This increase in the number of proletariat and the peasantry provided the nationalist leaders with more possible recruits.

The First World War itself also made this change in degree or scale more or less inevitable. First, the wholesale conscription of Africans during the war caused a great deal of anger and revulsion which did not disappear with the end of the war. Secondly, African soldiers fought alongside white soldiers and found out that the whites were no superior beings or supermen after all but just ordinary human beings who could be even more cowardly than the African and who could therefore be challenged after the war. Thirdly, both the ex-servicemen and those educated Africans who remained faithful to the colonial masters expected that they would be rewarded by some constitutional and social not to mention economic concessions after the war. But they were not, and this disappointment certainly fueled their postwar anticolonial activities. Moreover, the educated elite demanded that the principle of self-determination enunciated by Woodrow Wilson and others after the war should also apply to them. All this could not but intensity anticolonial activities.

Equally important were the economic conditions of the period. Unlike the earlier period, which was a period of economic boom and hence saw relatively limited anticolonial activities, the 1920s and 1930s were marked by a series of worldwide economic crises which caused prices of raw materials and cash crops to drop and those of manufactured goods to soar. The economic hardships created by these crises aroused a great deal of anger and made some people, both urban and rural, susceptible not only to anticolonial appeals but even more to the appeals of the new prophets and religious leaders, whose number proliferated during the period.

Finally, the Pan-Africanist activities of Sylvester Williams, Du Bois, Marcus Garvey, and others and their congresses in the metropolitan capitals — in Paris in 1919, London in 1920, Brussels and Paris in 1921, Lisbon in 1922, and New York in 1927 and, in the case of Garvey, in America and the West Indies — not only internationalized the anticolonial movement but also inspired the nationalists in Africa and won them some converts. The anticolonial activities of communist parties and groups after the October Revolution of 1917 also assisted the anticolonial cause. These activities culminated in the formation of the League against Imperialism and for National Independence at the International Congress sponsored by the Comintern at Brussels in February 1927. It is significant that this congress was attended by some Africans, including Jomo Kenyatta (Kenya), Lamine Senghor (West Africa), J. T. Gumede and La Guma (South Africa), and Messali Hadj and Hajali Abdel-Kader (Maghreb).

Not only do these factors explain the increase in intensity of anticolonial and nationalist activities, but it is against their background that African initiatives and reactions during the period should be examined.

As in the first period, the main objective of African nationalist activities between 1919 and 1935, both in the urban and rural areas, was usually not the overthrow but the reform of the colonial system. Again as in the former period, the channels for the articulation of African aspirations and grievances remained the former ones of associations, political movements and parties, and independent Ethiopian and Zionist churches. Only one new organization emerged during this period: trade unions. The main strategies in the urban areas remained rebellions, the use of the literary media, petitions to local and metropolitan governments, strikes, and boycotts. In the rural areas, the peasants and rural dwellers also continued their former strategies of revolts and uprisings, tax evasion, migration, flight or desertion, and peaceful resistance. The only difference was that with the sole exception of revolts and rebellions, which became less and less frequent, all the other channels and strategies increased qualitatively and quantitatively.

In the rural areas, some of the people and workers resorted to the old strategy of rebellions and insurrections. In South-West Africa, the Bondelswarts people rebelled against the increase in taxes in 1922, and aircraft had to be brought in before the rebellion was suppressed, at a cost of 100 Africans killed and more than 150 jailed.[26] In 1925, the Rehobothers not only rebelled but also petitioned the League of Nations regarding the harsh treatment they were receiving at the hands of the new South African government. But again machine guns and aircraft were moved in. In the Belgian Congo, many peasant rebellions broke out between 1920 and 1922 in the Bas-Congo region and in 1930 in the Kwango area. In 1931 there was a major uprising in the Kwilu Province by the Pende with the encouragement of the "prophet" Matemu-a-Kenenia over a steep increase in taxes and a 50 percent reduction in prices paid for farm commodities.

In Mozambique, the people of the Zambesi Valley, enraged by "forced labour, increased taxation, mandatory cotton production, sexual abuses and military conscription," actively participated in the rebellion organized by members of the Barue royal family and by the Shona spirit mediums which raged from 1917 till 1921. In the Sudan, the Mahdist uprisings continued till 1922, the most serious one being the Nyala revolt of 1922 in Darfur led by the *faki* Abdullah al-Sihayni with the aim of driving out the "infidels." In Southern Sudan, the Dinka under their prophet Ariendit and the Nuer led by their prophets Garluark and Guek Ngundeng also staged two very serious uprisings to end colonialism in 1919–20 and 1927–28, respectively; both revolts were suppressed with extreme brutality. There were also several local uprisings in Somaliland, especially Italian Somaliland, in 1920, 1922, 1925, 1927, 1932, 1935, and even in 1936.[28] In Nigeria there occurred what colonial historians have called the Aba women's riots of 1929, but it should be termed the Aba women's rebellion. This was touched off by the imposition of direct taxation and the introduction of new local courts and especially of warrant chiefs.

It should be emphasized, however, that not only were most of these rebellions very localized but they were also by and large confined mostly to the areas where governments were beginning to effectively consolidate their position after the First World War, as was clearly the case in South-West Africa, Somaliland, and Southern Sudan. In all the other areas of Africa, where effective occupation had been accomplished by the end of that war, Africans abandoned the violent strategy of the old leaders for a number of reasons. The first was that with the killing and exile of the old leaders, new leaders of the old stamp became fewer and fewer. Secondly, by the twenties most weapons had been confiscated, while gunpowder steadily disappeared from the open market. Finally, by the end of that war most African leaders had realized how absolutely futile any armed rebellion was.

Yet the rural folk did not, as a consequence of these factors, drop their resistance to colonialism. Rather, they shifted their emphasis from the use of violence to the less violent and well-known strategies of tax evasion, migration, flights or desertions, sabotage of machinery, and refusal to cultivate compulsory crops, as well as to the two apparently new strategies of boycotts and the dethronement of chiefs. In 1921, in protest against price fixing and the refusal of the European merchants to sell basic commodities on credit, the rural women of the Transkei area in South Africa organized a series of boycotts against European merchants. In Ghana, the cocoa farmers also organized a series of hold-ups and a boycott of imported European goods in 1920–21, 1930–31, and in 1937, precipitated partly by the worldwide economic crises of that period and the consequent sharp drop of cocoa prices.

A strategy resorted to more and more during this period, especially in the rural areas of East and Central Africa, was the use of the cultural symbols of dance, song, and art, which were often unintelligible to colonial officials.[29] In many East African colonies, dance associations were organized, and the associations created dance forms in which colonial officials were ridiculed. Not only did these associations become popular throughout eastern Africa, but they spread from there into the Belgian Congo after the First World War. Here, the associations, known as Mbeni, performed songs and dances that "often ridiculed European officials and expressed deep-seated popular resentment against colonial rule."[30] The Chope of southern Mozambique also developed a whole repertoire of songs in which the colonial regime in general and the hated tax officials in particular were denounced. Makua and Makonde artists ridiculed state officials in their carvings, in which they deliberately distorted their subjects' features. Many of these carvings can still be seen in the Museum de Nampula in Nampula. Though these cultural forms of resistance began before the First World War, they became more widespread afterwards.

Even more so than in the rural areas, the channels and strategies adopted by urban workers and the educated elite with very few exceptions remained virtually the same as those of the previous period, the only change being one of degree and intensity. As in the prewar period, the most important instruments of resistance were the associations and parties and the independent Ethiopian and Zionist churches, both of which proliferated throughout Africa. The main difference is that during this period a few more territorial and interethnic associations and movements emerged. The only completely new organization, and one that became increasingly important throughout the period, was the trade union. The strategies that these bodies adopted were the old literary ones of newspapers (whose numbers increased even more during this period), pamphlets, books, and petitions, and the more organized forms of delegations, political campaigns, strikes, and boycotts.

Numerous indeed were the elitist associations and groups which emerged after the war. They may be grouped into six main categories: improvement and welfare associations; social clubs; literary clubs; youth movements, or "young clubs," as they were known in East Africa; ethnic associations and unions; and political movements and parties. Let us briefly examine some of these elitist associations region by region, beginning with British West Africa.

In Ghana over fifty clubs and literary associations were formed, most of them between 1925 and 1930. In Nigeria the new associations included the Island Club of Lagos; the Nigerian Youth Movement, which was founded in 1934 and included all the young intellectuals of the day, such as H. O. Davies, Nnamdi Azikiwe, Dr. Vaughan, Dr. K. Abayomi, and Obafemi Awolowo; and numerous Igbo unions in such cities as Lagos, Abeokuta, and Ibadan. Among the political parties and movements that were formed in British West Africa were the Mambii party of Accra; the Nigerian National Democratic party of Nigeria, formed by Herbert Macaulay in 1923; and the most important and the most interesting of them all, the National Congress of British West Africa (NCBWA), formed in 1920. The NCBWA was the only territorial political movement that emerged in that area, and it had branches in all the British West African colonies — Nigeria, Ghana, Sierra Leone, and the Gambia.[31]

With one notable exception, none of these associations or parties demanded the overthrow of the colonial system. This is clearly borne out by the demands embodied in the eighty-two resolutions covering twelve topics passed by the NCBWA at its inaugural conference in Accra in 1920. These topics included administrative and legislative reforms, education, the question of aliens, banking and shipping, judicial reforms, the land question, and the question of self-determination. On the first topic, the members of the congress demanded a change in the constitutions of the British West African colonies "so as to give the people an effective voice in their affairs both in the Legislative and Municipal governments." They also demanded that the color bar be abolished in appointments to the civil service and that, in the future, admission be by competitive examination. In regard to education, they called for a British West African university to be set up "on such lines as would preserve in the students a sense of African nationality," and for compulsory education, presumably at the primary and secondary levels. On commerce and industry, they called for the repeal of the Palm Kernel Export Duty Ordinance and for measures to ensure the involvement of the people of the colonies in the promotion of the colonies' economic development. On judicial reforms, they insisted, among other things, that all judicial appointments be open to African lawyers of experience. On sanitary and medical reforms, they condemned racial discrimination in the medical service and demanded that the medical service be open to both blacks and whites and that entry be on the basis of competitive examinations. On the land issue, they condemned the compulsory acquisition of large areas of land at nominal rents. Finally on the topic of self-determination, they totally condemned the partitioning of Togo-land between Britain and France and the handing over of Camer-oons to the French "without consulting or regarding the wishes of the people in the matter."

It is interesting to note that all these resolutions ended on a typically conservative note in which the members of the congress placed on record "their attachment to the British connection and their unfeigned loyalty and devotion to the throne and person of His Majesty the King Emperor." Not only were most of these demands repeated at the subsequent conferences of the NCBWA in Freetown in 1923, Barthurst (now Banjul) in 1925–26, and Lagos in 1930, but they were practically the same as the demands made by the Gold Coast Youth Conference at its meeting in 1929 and by the Nigerian Youth Movement in 1934.

The only societies in the whole of British West Africa which demanded the immediate overthrow of the colonial system were the few branches of Garvey's UNIA in Ghana and Nigeria and the West African Youth League, founded in Ghana by Wallace Johnson. Wallace Johnson was a Sierra Leonean trade unionist who was trained in the Soviet Union in 1931–32 and upon his return to Ghana founded the Gold Coast Motor Car Union and the Gold Coast Workers' Protection Association in 1933 and the West African Youth League in 1934.[32] The aim of the league was to "champion the cause of the people and particularly the less favoured and down trodden [and] to defend the natural constitu-tional rights of the people of West Africa." In highly radical and inflammatory language, Wallace Johnson declared his readiness to use all possible means to fight for national self-determination of the "subjugated peoples of West Africa," and he campaigned for the overthrow of British rule in West Africa. As one would expect, the league soon gained a wide following among the youth and the workers. It is not surprising then, that the British arrested Wallace Johnson and deported him to his home country in 1938.

All these associations and clubs used the same old methods to press their demands: newspapers, petitions to the legislative councils, delegations to London (the NCBWA sent one to Lon-don in 1920), and numerous pamphlets and books written by such scholars as J. B. Danquah, Kobina Sekyi, and Azikiwe.[33]

However, in spite of all these demands and pressures, not much was achieved apart from the new constitutions introduced in Nigeria in 1922, in Sierra Leone in 1924, and in Ghana in 1925, which were all, as recent research has clearly shown, the direct outcome of the activities of the NCBWA. By the end of our period, therefore, British colonialism had been firmly entrenched in British West Africa.

In French West Africa, where nationalist or anticolonial activities were confined to Senegal and Dahomey, similar elitist and urban associations were active and made similar criticisms of colonialism and demands. In Senegal, the Young Senegalese Club and the Republican Socialist party continued their activities during this period, though the leader of the Republican Socialist party, Blaise Diagne, became mroe and more conservative in his demands; he died in 1934 an ardent defender of the colonial system. In Dahomey, the local branch of the Ligue des Droits de l'Homme and that of the Comité Franco-Musulman were revived by Hunkanrin after his repatriation from Paris in 1921. Unlike Diagne, Hunkanrin and his supporters resorted, in 1923, to a campaign of passive resistance against exorbitant taxes and high prices of imported goods, while workers went on strike and boycotted imported goods. This campaign was repressed with extreme violence, and Hunkanrin and all the other leaders were arrested and exiled to Mauritania, where all of them except Hunkanrin died. This repression ended radical anticolonial activities not only in Dahomey but throughout French West Africa during this period.

In East Africa, as in British West Africa, numerous organizations and associations emerged. The first of them to be formed during the period under review was the Young Baganda Association, organized in 1919 by Z. K. Sentongo, a noted pamphleteer. Its declared aims were "to improve Uganda in every way, to give a helping hand to deserved [sic] Muganda who may be in distress, [and] to settle the best way to enable us to get and maintain our education."[34] However, the association soon began to attack the colonial system and especially the Kabaka of Buganda and the chiefs as well as the Asians, whom it accused of exploiting the Africans. In Tanganyika the Tanganyika Territory African Civil Service Association was formed in 1922, and in 1929, the Tanganyika African Association, from which the Tanganyika African National Union (TANU) was formed twenty-five years later. In Kenya the Young Kavirondo Association was formed in 1921 by Jonathan Okiri, Jeremiah Awori, F. Omulo, and S. Syende, all of whom were teachers. Other east African associations were the Young Kikuyu Association, founded in 1921 by Harry Thuku and others, and the Kikuyu Central Association, formed in 1924 by Joseph Kangethe and James Beauttah, to whose secretaryship Jomo Kenyatta was appointed in 1928. A whole host of ethnic, welfare, and improvement associations — such as the Ukamba Members Association, the Kilimanjaro Native (coffee) Planters Association, and the Bukoba Bahayu Union — also appeared in Kenya, especially when Africans were not given representation on the Nairobi Municipal Council, established in 1928. As in British West Africa, there was only a single regional association in East Africa, the East African Association, founded in Nairobi in 1921 by Harry Thuku, a young Kikuyu civil servant and the first radical Kenya nationalist.[35]

Like the associations in West Africa, none of those in East Africa campaigned for independence but, rather, for the reform of the colonial system, and their demands were virtually the same as those of the West Africans, with more emphasis, of course, on land, labor, and various acts of discrimination. The Young Kavirondo Association, for instance, demanded the abolition of the *Kipande* (a pass), the reduction of the hut tax and poll tax and the exclusion of women from taxation, abolition of forced labor, and the building of a government school in central Nyanza. In a list of grievances presented to the governor in 1925, the Kikuyu Central Association (KCA) also called for the repeal of the Crown Lands Ordinance of 1915, which had made all African tenants at will of the Crown, protested the banning of the growing of cotton and coffee by Africans, and later demanded the building of a high school as well as a school for girls. Its new secretary, Jomo Kenyatta, appealed for cultural revival and established a Kikuyu-language newspaper, *Mwigwithania*, to win grass-roots support and lead the campaign for cultural revival.

However, using the old methods of petitions, newspaper campaigns, delegations to England, and pamphleteering, the East Africans, like their counterparts in West Africa, achieved hardly anything.

In central and southern Africa, among the new associations that emerged was the Rhodesian Bantu Voters Association, which was formed in 1923 "to aim and strive for the betterment of the Brown Race in school and Government."[36] It demanded greater voting rights for Africans and called for the return of seized lands. In Zambia the Mwenzo Welfare Association was founded in 1923 by David Kaunda, the father of Kenneth Kaunda; the association's aim was clearly stated to be not to subvert the government but rather to be "one of the helpful means of developing the country in the hands of the two necessary connecting links, the government and the governed." In Nyasaland the Mombera Native Association was formed in 1920. From the late 1920s Nyasaland "native associations" mushroomed. In 1933 alone, as many as fifteen were formed in the major cities of Zomba, Blantyre, Limo, Lilongwe, Fort Johnson, Karonga, and Chiraduzu. In Basutoland the Lekhotla la Bafo (League of the Poor) played a leading role in the anticolonial activities in that country. It condemned Britain for violating the protectorate agreement with the former king, Moshoeshoe.

In the Belgian Congo, no such associations emerged until the 1950s, and in Angola, only the two associations formed in the 1910s — the Liga Angolana, formed in 1913 by a few civil servants, and its breakaway offshoot, Gremio Africano — continued to operate. However, the leaders of these two associations, under attack by the authorities and fearful of losing their jobs, suspended their activities between the late twenties and the 1940s. Throughout this period, it was not associations but rather individual intellectuals, journalists, lawyers, and novelists, mainly mulatto, such as Antonio de Assis, Jr., who used the newspapers, poems, and novels to expose the abuses of colonialism. Similarly, while no associations emerged in Mozambique, the intellectuals used the newspapers, especially *O Brado Africano*, to level attacks on the colonial system. In the editorials, they constantly treated four main abuses: *chibalo* (forced labor), the poor working conditions of free African labor, the preferential treatment given to white immigrants, and the lack of educational opportunities. That there were almost no African elitist associations in the Belgian Congo, Angola, and Mozambique was due to a very limited access to secondary education in these areas before the Second World War.

In the whole of eastern, central, and southern Africa, only a single political party operated during this period, and that was the African National Congress in South Africa.[37] Though founded, as we have seen, in 1912, it was not until 1925 that it attained maturity and continental perspective, as was signified by the change of its name from the South African Native National Congress to African National Congress and the adoption of its now famous anthem "Nkosi Sikelel' i Afrika" (Lord, Bless Africa), and of its tricolor flag — black, green, and gold, signifying the black people, the green fields and veld, and the country's main mineral resource, respectively. From then on, it actively spearheaded the anticolonial movement not only in South Africa but throughout central and eastern Africa. In 1926, for instance, it organized a mass campaign against a new series of racist laws being introduced by James Hertzog, then prime minister of South Africa. In February 1926, it called a national convention in Bloemfontein which strongly condemned all racial segregation and demanded equality of all citizens irrespective of color. The ANC became rather inactive in the late 1920s and early 1930s, when its leadership was seized by moderates who were afraid of communist influence. But it bounced back again in the late thirties and has been in the forefront of the fight against racial discrimination and for the rights of the blacks in southern Africa ever since.

Besides these associations and political parties of the educated elite, the other main instruments of resistance to colonialism during the period were, as in the former period, the independent African churches. More Ethiopian and Zionist churches emerged in Africa, especially in southern and central Africa, during this period than in the previous one. The number of such churches in South Africa rose from 76 in 1918 to 320 by 1932 and to over 800 by 1942, and in Mozambique, from 76 in 1918 to more than 380 twenty years later.[38] The reasons for the increasing popularity of these churches are not far to seek. In the first place, the Ethiopian churches emphasized African self-improvement and political rights. Secondly, because of their very strong anticolonialism, many provided avenues to the ordinary people and peasants for the expression of their hostility to the new colonial sociopolitical system. Others also preached and promoted pride in African culture and exposed the hypocrisy of the established Christian churches for their condemnation of African culture, their subtle racial discrimination, and their collusion with the colonial oppressors. Above all, most of the leaders were charismatic and demagogic and could not but attract the masses, especially the oppressed, the displaced, and the fear-ridden.

A typical example of the separatist churches of the period in southern and central Africa was the Wellington movement, founded by Wellington Butelezi in the 1920s. Deriving his inspiration from a mixture of his apocalyptic vision and some form of Garveyism, he told his followers in the Transkei that American blacks in airplanes would come and help them liberate themselves from white domination. He was, of course, arrested and deported, but his movement continued and even spread.

The Kimbanguist and Kitawala churches, founded in the Lower Congo and Eastern Congo areas of the Belgian Congo in 1921 and 1923–25, were among the most powerful, widespread, and radical of the churches. The Kimbanguist Church was founded by Simon Kimbangu, a Bakongo catechist who declared himself an emissary of God sent to deliver Africans from colonial rule. Though Kimbangu was arrested on 14 September 1921 and exiled to Katanga, where he died thirty years later, his movement spread with astonishing speed throughout the Lower Congo basin. Equally widespread and radical was the Kitawala Church, also of the Watchtower or Zionist variety. It was founded by Tomo Nyirenda, among whose slogans were "Africa for Africans" and "Equality of Races." Begun in 1923 in the Katanga province, it had spread into Northern Rhodesia, Nyasaland, and

Tanganyika by 1926. Though Nyirenda escaped to Northern Rhodesia from the Congolese authorities in 1926, he was arrested by the British there and ultimately executed. But as was the case with Kimbanguism, the elimination of the prophet merely accelerated the spread of the movement in the 1930s. Its adherents helped to organize the 1931 boycott in Elizabethville and the strike of the Union Minière factory at Jadotville in 1936.

While many independent churches emerged in Mozambique — most of them introduced from neighboring South Africa and Rhodesia, or branches of the Kitawala and the Kumbanguist churches — very few were found in Angola. Among these few were the radical African Methodist Episcopal Church and the Missao Christa Ethiopia.

In East Africa not only independent churches but also some traditional religious cults arose to challenge the colonial system. While the Mumbo cult, founded in 1913, remained strong and active during this period, there were also new ones, like the cult founded by Ndonye wa Kauti in 1922 among the Kauba during a period of worldwide economic crisis. Many Watchtower churches were also established in East Africa, among them the Dini ya Roho (Holy Ghost) Church, founded among the Abaluyia of Kenya in 1927, and the Joroho (Holy Ghost) Church, founded by Alfoyo Odongo Mango among the Luo in 1932. In West Africa various Aladura churches of the Zionist or pentecostal variety were established. Other West African churches were the Apostolic Revelation Church and the Musama Disco Christo Church, both of Ghana, and the Negro Church of Christ; these are now categorized not as Ethiopian or Zionist but as indigenous churches whose sole purpose was to adapt Christianity to the culture and way of life of Africans.[39]

It was during this period that a new agency was added to the arsenal of the nationalists, and this was the organized trade union. One of the earliest and the most powerful to be founded in Africa was the Industrial and Commercial Workers Union (ICU) of South Africa. Recently described as "the largest African proletarian organisation," the ICU was founded by Clements Kadalie, a migrant teacher from Nyasaland, in January 1919 in Cape Town during a strike of African and colored workers. The union began with a membership of fewer than 30 people, but it had grown to 30,000 by 1924 and to 100,000 only three years later. Its main aim was to campaign for higher wages, better working conditions, pensions, and the like.

In East Africa, Angola, and Mozambique, trade-union activities were not allowed. In West Africa, though trade-union activities were not formally allowed till 1932 in the Gambia, 1939 in Sierra Leone and Nigeria, and 1941 in Ghana, some trade unions were formed nevertheless. The first trade union to be formed in British West Africa was the Railway Workers Union of Sierra Leone, founded in 1919. It was reorganized in 1925 to embrace both skilled and unskilled workers. The year 1919 also saw the formation of the Mechanics Union in Nigeria and the Native Defense Union in the Gambia.

The main strategies used by these unions, as well as by non-unionized workers throughout this period, were the usual ones of strikes and boycotts. Thus, in Sierra Leone, the Railway Workers Union organized a strike in 1920 for better wages and more humane treatment of workers, and another one in 1926 which lasted for six weeks. In Ghana, the Ashanti Goldfields Workers went on strike at Obuasi in 1924, while the Enugu coal miners in Nigeria and the workers on the Dakar–St. Louis railway struck in 1925. There were more numerous strikes in South Africa and in the Belgian Congo, especially in the area of the Katanga mines in the early 1930s. These strikes were instigated partly by the ICU and partly by the ANC and some of the independent African churches. Imported goods were boycotted because of their high prices in 1921, 1931, and 1937 in Ghana and in 1931 in Elizabethville in the Belgian Congo.

It should be obvious from the above that African resistance to colonialism, and the confrontation between the educated elite, the farm laborers, and the urban workers on one side and the colonial administrators and capitalist companies on the other, continued and assumed even wider dimensions between 1919 and 1935. Yet, on the eve of the Fascist occupation of Ethiopia, nowhere had these activities made any impression on the colonial system in Africa. Most of the educated nationalists, founders and leaders of independent African churches, and trade-union leaders had either been imprisoned or exiled or even killed. Most of the Ethiopian and Zionist churches had lost their dynamism by 1935, while even the ICU had attained the peak of its influence in the 1920s, and the ANC was in decline. In British West Africa, the NCBWA had also disappeared from the stage of history following the death of Casely Hayford in 1930; in East Africa, the great East African nationalist leader Harry Thuku, was in exile, and his East African Association had completely collapsed. By 1935, the colonial system looked virtually impregnable and seemed likely to last forever. Yet, it did not. Within forty-five years of the Italian occupation of Ethiopia, the colonial system had been wiped off the face of Africa except for southern Africa, and Africans had once more regained their sovereignty and independence, at least politically if not culturally and economically. How, then, can this unexpected turn of events be accounted for?

This question falls outside the scope of this book, but I shall answer it very briefly here, partly because the answers should be of great interest and partly to fill the gap between this chapter and the next, and final, one. The fall of the colonial system was due to five main factors: the Italian occupation of Ethiopia itself, the impact of the Second World War, the Pan-Africanist Congress of 1945 at Manchester, the formation of new political parties, and finally the emergence of new, dynamic, and radical African leaders who demanded this time not the reform of the colonial system but its total abolition and the restoration of African independence, sovereignty, and dignity.

The Italian occupation of Ethiopia was on the one hand the epilogue to or the last act of the long drama of the European Scramble for Africa and on the other the curtain-raiser to the new drama which ended in the sixties with the dismantling of colonialism in Africa.[40] In the first place, that event, which meant the snuffing out of the last symbol of African independence and black achievement, shocked and outraged not only politically conscious Africans at home and in Europe but also black people throughout the whole world and especially in the United States and the West Indies. Secondly, it ended any faith that moderate African leaders had in the progressive aspects of colonialism and convinced them of the need to overthrow that system. It seems evident from the mood of blacks throughout the world and that of educated West Africans and especially of people like Wallace Johnson, Nnamdi Azikiwe, Jomo Kenyatta, and Kwame Nkrumah that but for the outbreak of the Second World War, the revolution for independence would have been launched in the late thirties rather than in the late forties.

But if the Second World War delayed the revolutionary attack on the colonial system, it made that attack more or less inevitable in a number of ways. Many Africans were conscripted into the colonial armies, and this caused a great deal of anger in the colonial territories. Secondly, after being demobilized, the ex-servicemen expected certain rewards which never came. This made them more responsive to the anticolonial appeals of the nationalists, and many of them in fact became leaders and activists in the nationalist cause. Thirdly, and most important, the war left the colonial powers, especially France and Britain, impoverished and weak and therefore not too disposed to face up to the radical nationalists of the postwar period. All these factors therefore created a very favorable atmosphere for those nationalists.

The third factor leading to the eventual demise of the colonial system was the Pan-Africanist Congress at Manchester in 1945.[41] This congress — in which many future African leaders, such as Jomo Kenyatta and Kwame Nkrumah, actively participated — not only revived and rekindled interest in Pan-Africanism. It also called for the liberation of Africa from colonial rule and worked out strategies and tactics for accomplishing this end which some of the leaders later applied.

Fourth, the political parties that emerged after the war, unlike the earlier associations, which were elitist or bourgeois associations run by part-time officers, were parties organized along modern lines with party symbols, slogans, newspapers, propaganda machinery, and full-time officers. Above all, many of them were popular parties enjoying the support not only of the working classes and the masses but at times even of the traditional rulers. They therefore could no longer be ignored or easily bullied into submission, as the parties of the twenties and thirties were. Above all, the cry of these parties was "Self-Government

Now" (for the radicals) and "Self-Government Step by Step" (for the moderates), and not "Reform."

Finally, the leadership of these parties consisted mainly of people with very radical ideas who were ready to apply both constitutional and unconstitutional methods — or, as Nkrumah termed it, "positive action" — to achieve their ends. These men included Nnamdi Azikiwe and Obafemi Awolowo of Nigeria, Kwame Nkrumah of Ghana, Seku Ture of Guinea, Jomo Kenyatta of Kenya, Patrice Lumumba of the Belgian Congo, Hastings Kamuzu Banda of Nyasaland, Ahmed Ben Bellah of Algeria, and Gamal Abdal Nasser of Egypt. It was the dynamic and uncompromising leadership provided by these great sons of Africa that brought about the triumph of the final phase of the African nationalist and anticolonial activities, dating from the Fascist occupation of Ethiopia to the end of colonialism in the whole of Africa except southern Africa by 1980. Colonialism thus lasted in Africa from the 1880s to the 1970s. The question, then, is, What impact did it have on Africa? This question forms the subject of the final chapter.

CHAPTER FOUR

The Colonial Impact

A s we saw in the previous chapter, only forty-five years after the Italian occupation of Ethiopia, all African states except a few in southern Africa had been liberated politically from the yoke of colonialism, and Africans had regained their sovereignty and independence. In other words, nowhere in Africa did the colonial system last more than a hundred years — from the 1880s to the 1970s. In the history of a continent, a hundred years is a very brief span indeed, a mere episode or interlude in the life of the peoples. Yet, short and episodic as it was, there is no doubt that colonialism made an impact on the continent. In this final chapter, I would like to examine the nature of the legacies that colonialism has bequeathed to Africa, as well as assess the significance of colonialism for Africa and Africans.[1]

Nothing has become more controversial now than the question of the nature of the impact of colonialism on Africa. Many European and Eurocentric historians — such as L. H. Gann, P. Duignan, Margery Perham, P. C. Lloyd, and more recently D. K. Fieldhouse — have contended that the impact was both positive and negative, with positive aspects far outweighing the negative ones. Gann and Duignan, who appear to have devoted themselves to the defense of colonialism in Africa, concluded in 1967 that "the imperial system stands out as one of the most powerful engines for cultural diffusion in the history of Africa; its credit balance far outweighs its debit account."[2]

Other historians — mainly African, black, and Marxist scholars and especially the development and the underdevelopment theorists — have maintained that colonialism made no positive impact on Africa. The great exponents of this rather extreme position are Walter Rodney, the black Guianese historian and activist, and the Ugandan historian T. B. Kabwegyere. According to the former, "the argument suggests that, on the one hand, there was exploitation and oppression but on the other hand colonial governments did much for the benefit of Africans and they developed Africa. It is our contention that this is completely false. Colonialism had only one hand—it was a one-armed bandit."[3] Before deciding one way or the other, let us examine the colonial balance sheet in the political, social, and economic fields.

The first obvious positive political legacy was undoubtedly the establishment of continuous peace and stability in Africa, especially after the First World War. Let me hasten to add, first, that Africa was certainly not in a Hobbesian state of nature at the dawn of the colonial era and, secondly, that the first three decades of the colonial era, as should be obvious from the two previous chapters, introduced into Africa far more violence, instability, anarchy, and loss of African lives than probably any other period in its history. The population of the Belgian Congo fell by 50 percent, and that of the Herero by 80 percent, as a result of the oppressive and inhuman treatment of the Africans by the colonizers during the period. There is no doubt, however, that after the wars of occupation and the repression of African opposition and resistance, an era of continuous peace, order, and stability set in. This certainly facilitated and accelerated the economic and social changes that occurred on the continent during the colonial period.

The second positive political impact has been the very appearance of the independent African states of today. The partition of Africa by the imperial colonial powers led ultimately to the establishment of some forty-eight new states, most of them with clearly defined boundaries, in place of the existing innumerable lineage and clan groups, city-states, kingdoms, and empires without any fixed boundaries. It is significant that the boundaries of these states have been maintained ever since independence.

However, the creation of the states has proved to be more of a liability than an asset to the present independent African nations. Had the boundaries of these states been laid down in accordance with any well-defined, rational criteria and in full cognizance of the ethnocultural, geographical, and ecological realities of Africa, the outcome would have been wholesome. Unfortunately, many of these boundaries were arbitrarily drawn on African maps in the chancelleries of the imperial powers in Europe. The result has been that most of these states are artificial creations, and this very artificiality has created very serious problems, many of which have still not been solved. One of these problems is that of nation-state building. Because of the artificiality of these boundaries, each independent African state is made up of a whole host of different ethnocultural groups and nations having different historical traditions and cultures and speaking different languages. One can imagine, then, how stupendous the problem of developing the independent states of Africa into true nation-states is.

A second problem has been that of interstate boundary disputes. Not only did these artificial boundaries create multi-ethnic states, but worse still, they often run across preexisting nations, ethnicities, states, kingdoms, and empires. The Bakongo, for instance, are divided by the boundaries of the Congo, Zaire, Angola, and Gabon. Some of the Ewe live in Ghana, some in Togo, and others in Benin, while the Akan are found in the Ivory Coast and Ghana. The Somali are shared among Ethiopia, Kenya, and Somalia. The Senufo now live in Mali, the Ivory Coast, and Burkina Faso. Is it surprising, then, that there have been boundary disputes between Ghana and the Ivory Coast, Ghana and Togo, Burkina Faso and Mali, Nigeria and Cameroons, Somalia and Ethiopia, Kenya and Somalia, Sudan and Uganda?

A third problem has been the uneven sizes and unequal natural resources and economic potentialities of these states. Some of the states that emerged from the partition were really giants, like the Sudan, with an area of approximately 967,000 square miles, Zaire with 906,000, Algeria with 920,000, and Nigeria with 357,000; others were midgets, like the Gambia, with a total area of 4,000 square miles, and Lesotho and Burundi with 11,000 each. Moreover, some states have miles and miles of coastline, while others are landlocked, with no access to the sea. The latter include Mali, Burkina Faso, Niger, Chad, the Central African Re-

INDEPENDENT AFRICA

public, Uganda, Malawi, Zambia, Zimbabwe, and Botswana. Some have very fertile lands and several mineral resources, but others – such as Niger, Chad, and most of the Sudan, Algeria, and Egypt – are mere desert. Finally, while some states, like the Gambia and Somalia, have only a border or two to police, others have four or more, and Zaire has seven. Here, again, how can such handicapped states solve their problems of development? How can a state without access to the sea or without fertile land really develop? Can one imagine the problems of security and of smuggling confronting these states with so many borders to patrol?

The third positive political impact of colonialism was its introduction into Africa of two new institutions — a new bureaucracy
of civil servants and a new judicial system. On the first score, the
contribution of the Europeans was uneven: the British bequeathed a far better trained and numerically stronger civil service to its former colonies than the French, while the record of the
Belgians and the Portuguese is the worst in this field. However,
the judicial systems, bequeathed by the colonial administrations,
have not undergone any fundamental changes in any of the independent African states.

Another positive colonial impact was the generation of a sense
of nationalism as well as the intensification of the spirit of Pan-
Africanism. The colonial system generated a sense of identity and
consciousness among the different ethnic groups of each colonial
state, while the anticolonial literary activities of some of the educated Africans and more especially the Fascist attack on Ethiopia
and the connivance of the other European imperial powers diffused and strengthened the spirit of Pan-Africanism throughout
the black world.

But it should be immediately pointed out that African nationalism was one of the accidental by-products of colonialism. No
colonial power ever deliberately set out to generate or promote
that consciousness. Moreover, the nationalism that was generated by colonialism was not a positive but a negative one, arising
out of the sense of anger, frustration, and humiliation produced
by the oppressive, discriminatory, and exploitative measures and
activities of the colonial administrators. It is rather unfortunate
that with the overthrow of colonialism, this negative sentiment of
nationalism or, rather, anticolonialism has almost lost its cohe-
sive force. Independent African states are therefore now saddled
with the crucial problem of how to forge a new and more positive
force of nationalism in place of the negative one generated by colonialism, or, as Ali Mazrui and M. Tidy have recently put it,
how to move "from modern nationalism to modern
nationhood."[4]

Another political legacy bequeathed to independent African
states was the professional army. In traditional Africa, there were
hardly any full-time, standing armies. In the whole of West

Africa, it was probably only the kings of Dahomey and Samori Ture who developed real full-time, well-trained armies. However, all the imperial powers developed professional armies, which they used first to occupy and police their colonies, then in the First and Second World Wars, and finally in the campaigns against African independence; and these armies were among the most conspicuous legacies apart from physical structures bequeathed to independent African states. And what a legacy these armies have turned out to be! In retrospect, they have become nothing but a chronic source of instability, confusion, and anarchy as a result of their often unnecessary and unjustifiable interventions in the political processes of African countries. Indeed, African armies are the greatest millstones around the necks of African leaders, and the future of the continent is going to be determined very much on how these armies are dealt with.

The final political impact — and a very negative and regretable one — is the delay that colonialism caused in the political development and maturity of African states. If colonialism meant anything at all politically, it was the loss of sovereignty and independence by the colonized peoples. This loss of sovereignty, in turn, implied the loss of the right of a state to control its own destiny; to plan its own development; to decide which outside nations to borrow from or associate with or emulate; to conduct its own diplomacy and international relations; and above all, to manage or even mismanage its own affairs, derive pride and pleasure from its successes, and derive lessons, frustrations, and experience from its failures. As Rodney has pointed out, the seventy-year colonial era was one of the most dynamic and scientific periods in world history. It was the period, for instance, that witnessed Europe's entry into the age of the motor vehicle, of the airplane, and finally of nuclear power. Had African states been in control of their own destinies — as say, Japan was, or as South Africa became after 1910 — there is no reason why, judging from the very healthy and promising trends which were outlined in the first chapter, they could not also have followed the Japanese model, as indeed some of their educated sons, like Mensah Sarbah and the Malagasi scholar Ravelojaona, were advocating.[5] But colonialism completely isolated and insulated Africa from all these changes. It is in this loss of sovereignty and the consequent isolation from the outside world that one finds one of the most pernicious impacts of colonialism on Africa and one of the fundamental causes of its present underdevelopment and technological backwardness.

The impact of colonialism in the economic field, as in the political field, was clearly a mixed one. The most important economic benefit was the provision of an infrastructure of roads, railways, harbors, the telegraph and the telephone. The basic infrastructure of every modern African state was completed during the colonial period, and in most countries, not even a mile of railroad has been constructed since independence. A second important economic impact was the development of the primary sector of Africa's economy. It was during this period that the mineral potential of many African countries was discovered and modern scientific mining introduced. Above all, it was during this period that the production of such cash crops as cotton, peanuts, palm oil, coffee, tobacco, rubber, and cocoa, became the main feature of the political economy of many an African state.

These fundamental economic changes, in turn, had some far-reaching consequences. In the first place, land acquired great commercial value and assumed far greater importance than it had ever had before. Secondly, the spread of cash-crop agriculture enabled Africans of whatever social status, and especially rural Africans in many regions, to acquire wealth and raise their standard of living. Another significant impact was the spread and consolidation of the money economy in Africa and with it not only a change in the traditional standards of wealth and status but also a phenomenal increase (as will be seen below) in the class of wage earners and salaried persons. In the wake of the money economy came the banking activities which have become such a feature in the economies of independent African states. The sum total of all these colonial economic reforms was what has been described by economists as the completion of the integration of the African economy into the world economy in general and into the capitalist economy of the former colonial powers in particular.[6]

But the economic changes introduced by colonialism had a

negative side also. First, the transportation and communications infrastructure that was provided was not only inadequate but was also very unevenly distributed in nearly all the colonies. The roads and railways were by and large constructed to link areas with the potential for cash crops and with mineral deposits with the sea or the world commodity market. In other words, the infrastructures were meant to facilitate the exploitation of the natural resources but not to promote the accessibility and development of all regions of the colony. The outcome of this has been uneven regional economic development in most African countries, still a major stumbling block in the way of nation-building in Africa today.[7]

Secondly, the colonial system led to the delay of industrial and technological developments in Africa. As has been pointed out already, one of the typical features of the colonial political economy was the total neglect of industrialization and of the processing of locally produced raw materials and agricultural products in the colonies. It should not be forgotten that before the colonial period, Africans were producing their own building materials, their pottery and crockery, their soap, beads, iron tools, and especially cloth; above all, they were producing the gold that was exported to Europe and the Mediterranean world.[8] Had the traditional production techniques in all these areas been modernized and had industrialization been promoted, African industrial and technological development would have commenced much earlier than it did. But they were not. Instead, preexisting industries were almost all eradicated by the importation of cheap and even better substitutes from Europe and India, while Africans were driven out of the mining industry as it became an exclusive preserve of Europeans. This neglect of industrialization, destruction of the existing industries and handicrafts in Africa, and elimination of Africans from the mining field further explain Africa's present technological backwardness.

Thirdly, colonialism saddled most colonies with monocrop economies. During the colonial period, as may be recalled, each colony was made to produce a single cash crop or two, and no attempts were made to diversify the agricultural economy. The habit of producing these single cash crops appears to have become so ingrained that it has not been changed to any appreciable degree since independence. The other consequence of this concentration on the production of cash crops for export was the neglect of the internal sector of the economy and, in particular, of the production of food for internal consumption, so that rice, maize, fish, and other foods had to be imported. Thus, during the colonial period, Africans were encouraged to produce what they did not consume and to consume what they did not produce, a clear proof of the exploitative nature of the colonial political economy. It is lamentable that this legacy has not changed materially in most African countries. To this day, they have to rely on the importation of rice, maize, edible oil, flour, and other foodstuffs to survive.

Nor did the commercialization of land turn out to be an unqualified asset. In its trail followed a whole series of litigations over the ownership of land, which caused widespread poverty, especially among the ruling houses and land-owning families. Again, litigation over land has continued to this day.

Colonialism also put an end to inter-African trade. I pointed out in the first chapter that on the eve of the imperial scramble and occupation, the commercial unification of the African continent had been completed. There is no doubt that Africans would have continued to trade among themselves as they had been doing from time immemorial. One of the consequences of this interregional and intraregional trade would have been the continuing spread of, say, the Swahili language and culture in eastern and central Africa, the Hausa language and culture in western Africa, and the Arabic language and culture in northern Africa. What a beneficial development this would have been for the whole continent! But colonialism put an end to all this. The new artificial boundaries not only divided peoples but also blocked the centuries-old transregional and regional caravan routes. Trading between even members of the same ethnic group on either side of new borders suddenly became no longer trading but smuggling, which was heavily punished. On the contrary, the flow of trade in each colony was now oriented to the relevant metropolitan country. The sad thing is that even after twenty years of independence, this orientation has not ended, thanks to the neocolonialist activities of the former metropolitan countries and their African allies.

Finally, the monetary policies pursued by all the colonial powers must be held partly responsible for the present underdeveloped state of the continent. Under these policies, all the colonial currencies were tied to those of the metropolitan countries, and all their foreign exchange earnings were kept in the metropolitan countries and not used for internal development. The expatriate commercial banks and companies were also allowed to repatriate their deposits, savings, and profits instead of reinvesting them in the colonies for further development. The consequence of all this was that at the time of independence, no African state apart from the Union of South Africa had the strong economic or industrial base needed for a real economic takeoff. And if this base could not be provided during the eighty-year period of colonial rule, should we expect it to have been done in twenty years of independence, especially in the light of the changing international economic order?

What about the impact in the social field? Here again, there are both credit and debit sides. In the first place, there is no doubt that after the initial decline, population growth resumed after the First World War. Caldwell has estimated that the population of Africa increased by 37 percent during the colonial period. The increase was undoubtedly due to some of the policies and activities of the colonial administrators — such as the provision of roads and railways, which made for mobility; the campaign launched against such epidemic diseases as sleeping sickness, bubonic plagues, yellow fever, and yaws; and the provision of some medical facilities.

A second important benefit was urbanization. Not only did preexisting towns expand, but completely new urban centers emerged following the establishment of the colonial system. The new cities included Abidjan in the Ivory Coast, Takoradi in Ghana, Port Harcourt and Enugu in Nigeria, Nairobi in Kenya, Salisbury (now Harare) in Zimbabwe, Lusaka in Zambia, and Luluabourg in Zaire. All these new urban centers were created either as ports or harbors, mining centers, administrative centers, or railway centers or terminuses. The population of Nairobi, which was founded in 1896 as a transit depot for the construction of the Uganda railway, rose from 13,145 in 1927 to over 25,000 by 1940; that of Accra jumped from 17,892 in 1901 to 135,926 in 1948; and that of Casablanca, from 2,026 in 1910 to 250,000 in 1936.[9] There is no doubt that the quality of life for Africa's population was relatively improved through the provision of piped water, hospitals and dispensaries, better housing and sanitary facilities.

A third important social benefit of colonialism was the spread of Christianity and Islam and especially of Western education. During the colonial period Christianity gained far more converts and penetrated farther, especially in East and Central Africa, than it had in all the previous three or four centuries put together. Islam also gained a lot of ground thanks to the patronage especially of the French and British colonial administrators. It should be emphasized that traditional African religion maintained its position in the face of all the inroads by these foreign religions.

The spread of Western education was due mainly to the activities of the Christian missionaries. By the 1930s, there were very few areas in Africa where elementary education was not being provided, while a few secondary schools and, from the 1940s onwards, even universities began to appear everywhere except in the Portuguese and Belgian colonies. The impact of Western education on African societies is too well-known to be discussed here. Suffice it to say that it was mainly responsible for producing the educated African elite which not only spearheaded the overthrow of the colonial system but also constitutes the backbone of the civil service of independent African states.

The other beneficial result of the spread of Western education was the provision of a lingua franca for each colony or cluster of colonies. In all the colonies, the mother tongue of the metropolitan country became the official language as well as the main medium of communication among the multi-ethnic populations of each colony. With very few exceptions (Tanzania, Kenya, Madagascar, and the states of North Africa), the metropolitan languages are to this day the official and business languages in Africa.

The final social benefit was the new social order that emerged in Africa as a result of the operation of the colonial system. Though there was social mobility in the traditional African social order, undue weight was given to birth. The colonial system, on the other hand, emphasized individual merit and achievement rather than birth, and this greatly facilitated social mobility. Moreover, as a result of Western education, employment opportunities, the production of cash crops, the abolition of slavery, and many other new avenues for advancement, all introduced by colonialism, a new social structure emerged. In place of the traditional structure of ruling aristocracy, ordinary people, and slaves, by the 1930s a new structure had developed, divided, first, into rural and urban dwellers, and then further subdivided. The urban dwellers became stratified into three main subgroups: namely, the elite, or, as others would term them, the administrative-clerical-professional bourgeoisie; the nonelite, or subelite; and the urban proletariat, or workers. The rural population became subdivided into a rural proletariat, or landless peasantry, especially in southern and eastern Africa, and peasants. The social order produced by the colonial system has been maintained, and the stratification has been, if anything, sharpened even further since independence. I regard this new social structure as an asset because membership is based on individual effort and achievement rather than on birth.

It would appear that the positive contribution of colonialism in the social field was quite considerable. Unfortunately, so also — and probably more so — was the negative impact. In the first place, it was the colonial system that initiated the gap that still exists between the urban and rural areas. All of the modern facilities — schools, hospitals, street lights, radio, postal services — and above all most of the employment opportunities were concentrated in the urban centers. The combination of modern life and employment pulled rural dwellers, especially the young ones and those with schooling, in the direction of the cities.

Secondly, the social services provided by colonialism were

grossly inadequate and unevenly distributed. For instance, while in Nigeria by the 1930s, twelve modern hospitals had been built for Europeans, who numbered only 4,000, there were only fifty-two for Africans, numbering 40 million. In Dar es Salaam the ratio of beds to population by 1920 was approximately 1 to 10 for the European hospital and 1 to 400–500 for the African hospital.

There was even greater deficiency, uneven distribution, and in this case even misdirected orientation in the educational facilities that were provided in colonial Africa. University education was totally ignored in all the colonies until the 1940s, and only one university was subsequently established for each colony. In Portuguese Africa, there were no universities. Moreover, most of the secondary schools were in the major cities and the coastal areas of the colonies and seldom in the interior and rural regions. Thirdly, in no colony was the demand for education at all levels ever adequately met. In practically every colony, only a very small percentage of school-age children could gain admission into schools. Educational facilities were so limited and so unevenly distributed simply because education was not really meant for the benefit of the Africans themselves but primarily "to produce Africans who would be more productive for the [colonial] system."[10] Nor were the curricula provided by these educational institutions of real relevance to the needs and aspirations of Africans. Most of the curricula were in fact carbon copies of those of the metropolitan countries.

The effects of colonial education were really unfortunate. First, because of its inadequacy, large numbers of Africans remained illiterate, and illiteracy is still widespread. Secondly, the elite produced by these colonial educational institutions were with few exceptions people who were alienated from their own society in terms of their dress, outlook, and tastes in food, music, and even dance. They were people who worshiped European culture, equating it with civilization, and looked down upon their own culture. Radical African scholars are now talking of colonial mis-education rather than education. Unfortunately, it is this very alienated and badly oriented elite that have dominated both the political and the social scene in Africa since independence. Above all, the neglect of technical education and the emphasis on liberal education created in educated Africans a contempt for manual work and an admiration for white-collar jobs which have still not left them. Finally, the use of the metropolitan language as the lingua franca also had the most regrettable effect of preventing the development of an official African language as a lingua franca in each colony or even in a cluster of colonies. This question has become so sensitive that only a few African states have been able to tackle it since independence.

Another negative social impact of colonialism was the downgrading of the status of women in Africa. During the colonial period, there were far fewer facilities for girls than for boys. Women could therefore not gain access into the professions — medicine, law, the civil service, and the bench. Very few women were ever appointed to any "European post," while there was never a female governor of a colony. The colonial world was definitely a man's world, and women were not allowed to play any meaningful role in it except as petty traders and farmers.

The colonial administrators and their allies, the European missionaries, condemned everything African in culture — African names, music, dance, art, religion, marriage, the system of inheritance — and completely discouraged the teaching of all these things in their schools and colleges. Even the wearing of African clothes to work or school was banned. All this could not but retard the cultural development of the continent. One of the greatest achievements of independent African governments has been the revival of and the generation of pride in African culture and its propagation in the outside world.

But the last and the most serious negative impact of colonialism has been psychological. This is seen, first, in the creation of a colonial mentality among educated Africans in particular and also among the populace in general. This mentality manifests itself in the condemnation of anything traditional, in the preference for imported goods to locally manufactured goods (since independence), and in the style of dress — such as the wearing of three-piece suits in a climate where temperatures routinely exceed eighty degrees Fahrenheit. Above all, it manifests itself in the belief so prevalent among Africans, both literate and illiterate, that government and all public property and finance belong, not to the people, but to the colonial government, and could and should therefore be taken advantage of at the least opportunity, a belief which leads to the often reckless dissipation and misuse of public funds and property.

Another psychological impact is apparent in ostentatious and flamboyant life-styles, especially on the part of the elite and businessmen. All this arose from the fact that while the colonialists taught their colonial subjects the Protestant work ethic, the drive for worldly success, and the acquisitive instinct, they did not, for obvious reasons, inculcate in them the puritanical spirit which emphasized frugality and very little consumption. In other words, colonialism taught its subjects only part of the puritanical lesson of "make money," not the full one of "make money but do not spend it," which, according to Ali Mazrui, "seemed to be the ultimate commercial imperative operating within the Protestant ethic."[11] Thus, while in Europe this full ethic led to the rise of capitalism, as both Weber and Tawney have clearly shown, and with it the scientific and technological breakthrough, in the African colonies it only generated the ostentatious consumption habits which are still very much with us.

The final and worst psychological impact has been the generation of a deep feeling of inferiority as well as the loss of a sense of human dignity among Africans. Both complexes were surely the outcome not only of the wholesale condemnation of everything African already referred to but, above all, of the practice of racial discrimination and the constant humiliation and oppression to which Africans were subjected throughout the colonial period. The sense of human dignity seems to have been regained, but the feeling of inferiority has not entirely disappeared even after two decades of independence.

It should be obvious from the above, then, that all those historians who see colonialism as a "one-armed bandit" are totally wrong. Equally guilty of exaggeration are those colonial apologists who see colonialism as an unqualified blessing for Africa as well as those who see its record as a balanced one. Colonialism definitely did have its credit and debit sides, but quite clearly the debit side far outweighs the credit side. Indeed, my charge against colonialism is not that it did not do anything for Africa, but that it did so little and that little so accidentally and indirectly; not that the economy of Africa under colonialism did not grow but that it grew more to the advantage of the colonial powers and the expatriate owners and shareholders of the companies operating in Africa than to the Africans; not that improvements did not take place in the lives of the African peoples but that such improvements were so limited and largely confined to the urban areas; not that education was not provided but that what was provided was so inadequate and so irrelevant to the needs and demands of the African themselves; not that there was no upward social mobility but that such a relatively small number of Africans did get to the top. In short, given the opportunities, the resources, and the power and influence of the colonial rulers, they could and should have done far more than they did for Africa. And it is for this failure that the colonial era will go down in history as a period of wasted opportunities, of ruthless exploitation of the resources of Africa, and on balance of the underdevelopment and humiliation of the peoples of Africa.

What then is the real significance of colonialism for Africa? Was it just a mere interlude that did not and will not affect the course of African history, or has it left an indelible imprint on Africa which is destined to influence its future? This topic has become a very controversial one. To a majority of historians, colonialism, though a short period in the history of Africa, is of great significance and bound to affect the future course of events. As Oliver and Atmore contend, "Measured on the time-scale of history, the colonial period was but an interlude of comparatively short duration. But it was an interlude that radically changed the direction and momemtum of African history." To Gann and Duigan, the colonial era was "the most decisive for the future of Africa."[12]

The other school of thought, championed by scholars such as Ajayi and Hopkins, regards the impact of colonialism on Africa as skin-deep, seeing colonialism as a mere episode that did not constitute any break with the African past. Ajayi has argued out this case in a series of articles, while Hopkins has also maintained that "colonial rule itself had a less dramatic and a less pervasive economic impact than was once supposed," that colonialism did "not create modernity out of backwardness by suddenly disrupting a traditional state of low-level equilibrium," and that "the main function of the new rulers was to give impetus to a process of economic development which was already under way."[13] Ali Mazrui has recently placed his enormous weight behind this school of thought. As he and Tidy have recently concluded, "The impact of the West may now turn out to be more short-lived than many have expected."[14]

I believe that the issue at stake is not as clear-cut and simple as both schools of thought have made it look. In some respects the impact of colonialism was deep and certainly destined to affect the future course of events, but in others, it was not. For instance, the colonial impact in the economic field was on the whole decisive and fundamental and affected both the rural and urban areas. In virtually all parts of Africa, the money economy completely and permanently replaced the barter economy. With the use of cash, the status of the individual in society came to be and is still determined by the amount of money or personal property that he has been able to accumulate, not by his birth or age or the number of his wives and children. Likewise, the commercialization of land which followed the introduction of cash crops and the modern mining industry has remained and is growing in intensity each day. Again, the integration of the economy of Africa into the world economy in general and into that of the former colonial powers in particular is destined to remain forever in the case of the world economy and for a very long time in the case of the European economies.

Many aspects of the political impact of colonialism are going to be even more lasting. In the first place, the very appearance of the present political map of Africa is a direct product of colonialism, and with the adoption of the principle of the sanctity of national boundaries by the Organization of African Unity (OAU), this appearance is going to endure. Secondly, the fundamental shift of the focus of political authority and power from the old ruling aristocracy of kings and priests to the educated elite (or, as Chinweizu insists on calling them, the petite bourgeoisie)[15] is also going to remain. Finally, the colonial armies which were bequeathed to African states have been and are certainly going to be maintained for a considerable length of time. These armies have already played crucial and in many cases disastrous and negative roles in the political processes in independent African states, and it appears that their role is not yet ended. In all these ways, then, the impact of colonialism in the political field was crucial and will prove of lasting consequence.

In the cultural field, the colonial impact has already proved to be superficial and ephemeral. Most of the changes that were introduced in this area, such as racial discrimination and the condemnation of African culture, have disappeared with the attainment of independence. Today, African art, music, and dance are recognized and taught in most of the institutions of higher learning both in and outside Africa, and exhibitions of African art have taken place in most of the capitals and major cities of the world since independence.

Finally, some aspects of the social impact will also endure. The foreign linguae francae are going to remain with us for a very long time if not forever. The new social classes produced by colonialism are bound to remain and will probably grow in complexity. Indeed, two new groups have already emerged since independence. The first consists of the new political elite of the leading members of the political parties that mushroomed in Africa during and since the independence revolution. Members of this group include former and current presidents, prime ministers, ambassadors, and high commissioners. The second is the military elite of the present and former officers of the armed forces of each independent state. Finally, the formation of independent African churches which began during the colonial era has continued and in fact has greatly intensified since independence.

In the light of all the above, we may safely conclude that though colonialism was a mere episode lasting no more than a hundred years anywhere in Africa, it was nonetheless an extremely important one. It marks a clear watershed in the history of the continent, and Africa's subsequent development is bound to be very much determined by some of its legacies. Ali Mazrui has recently speculated that "African culture may reclaim its own and help Africa retreat back to its ancestral authenticity, or Africa may struggle to find a third way."[16] I do not agree with the first alternative, since any such retreat is exceedingly unlikely if not utterly impracticable. I find the second alternative more realistic, but even here, I am convinced that any third way that would be found would still bear some of the impregnations and scars of colonialism. It would be most expedient, then, for African leaders to take the colonial impact very much into account in the formulation of their future development programs and strategies.

Notes

Preface

1. L. H. Gann and P. Duignan, *Burden of Empire* (London; Pall Mall, 1967); L. H. Gann and P. Duignan, eds., *Colonialism in Africa*, 5 vols. (Cambridge: Cambridge University Press, 1969); *The Cambridge History of Africa*, 8 vols. (Cambridge: Cambridge University Press, 1976); D. K. Fieldhouse, *Colonialism, 1870–1945: An Introduction*, (London: Weidenfeld and Nicolson, 1981); and P. Gifford and R. W. Louis, eds., *Britain and France in Africa* (New Haven: Yale University Press, 1971); and *Britain and Germany in Africa* (New Haven: Yale University Press, 1967).
2. A. Adu Boahen, ed., *General History of Africa*, vol. 7, UNESCO (London: Heinemann, 1985). Hereafter cited as *UNESCO History*.

CHAPTER ONE The Eve of the Colonial Conquest and Occupation

1. J. Dupuis, *Journal of a Residence in Ashantee*, new ed. (London: Frank Cass, 1966), pp. 162–64.
2. P. Curtin, S. Feierman, L. Thompson, and J. Vansina, *African History* (London, Longman, 1978), pp. 418–43.
3. A. A. Boahen, *Britain, the Sahara, and Western Sudan* (Oxford: Clarendon Press, 1964), pp. 103–4.
4. Curtin et al., *African History*, pp. 419–20.
5. Ibid., p. 420.
6. For details of these developments see P. J. Vatikiotis, *The Modern History of Egypt* (London: Weidenfeld and Nicolson, 1969), and M. Crowder, *West Africa under Colonial Rule* (London: Hutchinson, 1971).
7. For the full text of the constitution, see J. E. Casely Hayford, *Gold Coast Native Institutions*, new ed. (London: Frank Cass, 1970), pp. 327–40. See also H. S. Wilson, ed., *Origins of West African Nationalism* (London: Macmillan, 1969), pp. 213–18.
8. Casely Hayford, *Gold Coast Native Institutions*, p. 329.
9. Ibid., p. 187.
10. Ibid.

11. J. A. Horton, *West African Countries and Peoples,* new ed. (Edinburgh: Edinburgh University Press, 1964), p. 151.
12. A. Pallinder-Law, "Aborted Modernization in West Africa," *Journal of African History* 15 (1974): 65–82.
13. Ibid.
14. I. C. Caldwell, "The Social Repercussions of Colonial Rule: Demographic Aspects," in Boahen, *UNESCO History,* 7:483.
15. J.F.A. Ajayi and S. A. Akintoye, "Yorubaland in the Nineteenth Century," in O. Ikime, ed., *Groundwork of Nigerian History* (Ibadan: Heinemann, 1980), p. 300.
16. For details of these jihads, see J.F.A. Ajayi and M. Crowder, *History of West Africa,* 2 (London: Longman, 1974): 1–29, and M. Hisket, *The Development of Islam in West Africa* (London: Longman, 1984).
17. On this subject, see R. Oliver, *The Missionary Factor in East Africa* (London: Longman, 1965); A. J. Willis, *An Introduction to the History of Central Africa* (London: Oxford University Press, 1964); E. Roux, *Time Longer than Rope,* 2d ed. (Madison: University of Wisconsin Press, 1964); and J.F.A. Ajayi, *Christian Missions in Nigeria* (London: Longman, 1965).
18. Curtin et al., *African History,* p. 414.
19. M. Wilson and L. Thompson, eds., *The Oxford History of South Africa* vol. 2, (Oxford: Clarendon Press, 1971), pp. 74–75.
20. Leo Kuper, "African Nationalism in South Africa, 1910–1964," in ibid., 2:433–34.
21. Roux, *Time Longer than Rope,* pp. 53–80; E. Walker, *A History of Southern Africa,* 3d ed. (London: Longman, 1957), pp. 50, 394, 521, 536.
22. E. Ayandele, *The Missionary Impact on Modern Nigeria, 1842–1914: A Political and Social Analysis* (London: Longman, 1966), pp. 185–96.
23. C. M. Fyle, *The History of Sierra Leone* (London: Evans Brothers, 1981), pp. 74–6; Ayandele, *The Missionary Impact,* pp. 53–9, 192–200; R. W. July, *The Origins of Modern African Thought* (London: Faber, 1967), pp. 110–374; Boahen, *UNESCO History,* 7:700.
24. M. Morsy, *North Africa, 1800–1900* (London: Longman, 1984), pp. 233–45.
25. G. Shepperson and T. Price, *Independent African* (Edinburgh: Edinburgh University Press, 1958), pp. 72–74; Roux, *Time Longer than Rope,* pp. 77–80; B.G.M. Sundkler, *Bantu Prophets in South Africa,* 2d ed. (London: Oxford University Press, 1961), pp. 38–47; D. B. Barrett, ed., *African Initiatives in Religion* (Nairobi: East African Publishing House, 1971), pp. 18–24.
26. A. Horton, *West African Countries and Peoples,* new ed. (Edinburgh: Edinburgh University Press, 1964); *Letters on the Political Condition of the Gold Coast,* 2d ed. (London: Frank Cass, 1970); *Physical and Medical Climate and Meteorology of the West Coast of Africa* (London: Churchill, 1876).
27. Horton, *West African Countries,* pp. 69 and ix–x.
28. Horton, *Letters on the Political Condition,* p. i.

29. G. Shepperson, Introduction to Horton, *West African Countries,* p. xvii.
30. For Blyden's biography, see H. R. Lynch, *Edward Wilmot Blyden* (London: Oxford University Press, 1967). See also J. C. Coleman, *Nigeria: Background to Nationalism* (Berkeley and Los Angeles: University of California Press, 1958), pp. 106-7, 175-6, 183-4, and July, *Origins of Modern African Thought,* pp. 208-33.
31. Quoted by Wilson, *Origins of West African Nationalism,* pp. 239-40.
32. Ibid., pp. 249-50.
33. Ayandele, *The Missionary Impact,* pp. 187, 195-6.
34. Boahen, *UNESCO History,* 7:700; Morsy, *North Africa,* pp. 119-22.
35. Quoted by B. Davidson, *The African Past* (London: Longman, 1964), pp. 357-8.
36. Quoted by J. Fynn in M. Crowder, ed., *West African Resistance* (London: Hutchinson, 1971), pp. 43-44.
37. Quoted by I. G. Wilks in *Asante in the Nineteenth Century* (Cambridge: Cambridge University Press, 1975), p. 588.
38. Quoted by J. D. Hargreaves, "The French Conquest of Dahomey," *History Today* 30 (March 1980): 5-9.
39. Quoted by T. O. Ranger in Boahen, *UNESCO History* 7:49.
40. Quoted by A. Isaacman, *Anti-Colonial Activity in the Zambesi Valley, 1850-1921* (Berkeley and Los Angeles: University of California Press, 1976), pp. 128-29.
41. Quoted by M. Crowder in *West Africa under Colonial Rule* (London: Hutchinson, 1968), p. 97.
42. Quoted in Boahen, *UNESCO History,* 7:4.
43. A. G. Marcus, *The Life and Times of Menelik II* (Oxford: Clarendon Press, 1975), p. 160.
44. M. Perham, *The Colonial Reckoning* (London: Collins, 1961), p. 32.

CHAPTER TWO The Imposition of the Colonial System: Initiatives and Responses

1. See J. Schumpeter, *Imperialism and Social Classes* (Cleveland: World Publishing Co., 1955); R. E. Robinson and J. Gallagher, *Africa and the Victorians* (London: Macmillan, 1961); J. A. Hobson, *Imperialism: A Study* (Ann Arbor: University of Michigan Press, 1965); J. S. Keltie, *The Partition of Africa* (London: E. Stanford, 1893); V. I. Lenin, *Imperialism: The Highest Stage of Capitalism* (Moscow: Progress Publishers, 1983); A. G. Hopkins, *An Economic History of West Africa* (London: Longman, 1973); G. N. Uzoigwe, *Britain and the Conquest of Africa* (Ann Arbor: University of Michigan Press, 1974); B. I. Obichere, *West African States and European Expansion* (New Haven: Yale University Press, 1971); J. D. Hargreaves, *Prelude to the Partition of West Africa* (London: Macmillan, 1963); B. Sutcliffe and R. Owen, eds., *Studies in the Theory of Imperialism* (London: Longman, 1972); W. Rodney, *How Europe Underdeveloped Africa*

(Dar es Salaam: Tanzania Publishing House, 1972); Chinweizu, *The West and the Rest of Us* (New York: Vintage Books, 1975); D. K. Fieldhouse, *Colonialism, 1870–1945*,

2. Hopkins, *Economic History of West Africa*, pp. 165–66.
3. I. A. Asiwaju, Professor of History, University of Lagos, paper presented at the Nigerian National Open University.
4. W. D. McIntyre, *The Imperial Frontier in the Tropics, 1865–1875* (London: Macmillan, 1967).
5. C.J.H. Hayes, *A Generation of Materialism, 1871–1900*, (New York: Harper and Row, 1941), pp. 205–8.
6. Lenin, *Imperialism*, p. 80.
7. Fieldhouse, *Colonialism*.
8. J. A. Hobson, *Imperialism: A Study*, new ed. (Ann Arbor: University of Michigan Press, 1965).
9. M.H.Y. Kaniki, ed., *Tanzania under Colonial Rule* (London: Longman, 1980), p. 69.
10. Boahen, *UNESCO History*, 7:27–29.
11. A. S. Kanya-Forstner, "Mali-Tukulor," in Crowder, *West African Resistance*, pp. 53–79; A.J.P. Taylor, *Germany's Bid for Colonies* (London: Macmillan, 1938).
12. S. E. Crowe, *The Berlin–West African Conference* (London: Longmans Green, 1942).
13. Boahen, *UNESCO History*, 7:29–31.
14. S. Touval, "Treaties, Borders, and the Partition of Africa," *Journal of African History* 7 (1966): 279–92.
15. Hargreaves, *Prelude to the Partition of West Africa*, pp. 253–349; Kanya-Forstner, "Mali-Tukulor," pp. 53–79.
16. A. B. Davidson, "African Resistance and Rebellion against the Imposition of Colonial Rule," in T. O. Ranger, ed., *Emerging Themes of African History* (Nairobi: East African Publishing House, 1968), pp. 177–188.
17. See the *Gold Coast Times*, the *Gold Coast Chronicle*, the *Methodist Herald*, and the *Sierra Leone Weekly News* for these years.
18. Quoted by Lynch in *Edward Wilmot Blyden*, p. 197.
19. Boahen, *UNESCO History*, 7:197–98.
20. Crowder, *West Africa under Colonial Rule*, p. 72.
21. Ghana National Archives, Ferguson's Report of 1892.
22. M. Perham and M. Bull, eds., *The Diaries of Lord Lugard*, vol. 2 (Evanston, Ill.: Northwestern University Press, 1963).
23. Boahen, *UNESCO History*, 7:205–7, 268–70.
24. Ibid., pp. 134–35.
25. Ibid., p. 211.
26. Crowder, *West African Resistance*, pp. 69–77.
27. R. Oliver and J. D. Fage, *A Short History of Africa* (Harmondsworth: Penguin, 1962), p. 203.
28. For a detailed discussion of this issue, see A. A. Boahen, "Towards a New Categorization and Periodization of African Responses and Reactions to

Colonialism" (seminar paper, Department of History, University of Ghana, 1976).

29. Ibid.

30. Kanya-Forstner, "Mali-Tukulor," p. 69.

31. Ibid., and Y. Saint-Martin, *L'empire toucouleur et la France* (Dakar, 1972), p. 381.

32. S. Marks, "Khoisan Resistance to the Dutch," *Journal of African History* 13 (1972): 55–80; J. Thornton, "The State in African Historiography," *Ufahamu* 4, no. 2 (1973): 119–20.

33. Quoted by I. G. Wilks, *Asante in the Nineteenth Century* (Cambridge: Cambridge University Press, 1975), p. 640.

34. Ibid., pp. 644–45.

35. Quoted by A. A. Boahen, "Prempeh in Exile," *Research Review* (Legon) 8 (1977): 3–20.

36. For a detailed discussion of the initiatives and resistance of these African kings and rulers, see chaps. 4–11 of vol. 7 of the *UNESCO History*; the section here is more or less a summary of these chapters.

37. Quoted by D.J.M. Muffett in Crowder, *West African Resistance*, pp. 284–87.

38. For the details of this heroic and fascinating story, see Y. Person, *Samori*, 3 vols., (Paris: Mém de l'IFAN, 1968–75); Y. Person, "Guinea-Samori," in Crowder, *West African Resistance*, pp. 121–6; Boahen, *UNESCO History*, 7:123–27.

39. Person, "Guinea-Samori," in Crowder, *West African Resistance*, p. 136.

40. Wilks, *Asante in the Nineteenth Century*, pp. 301–5.

41. Ibid., p. 304.

42. T. C. Weiskel, *French Colonial Rule and the Baule Peoples, 1889–1911* (Oxford: Clarendon Press, 1980), pp. 98–102.

43. For details of this unique story of success see S. Rubenson, *Wuchale XVII: The Attempt to Establish a Protectorate over Ethiopia* (Addis Ababa: Haile Selassie I University, 1964); H. G. Marcus, *The Life and Times of Menelik II* (Oxford: Clarendon Press, 1975); R. Greenfield, *Ethiopia: A New Political History* (New York: Praeger, 1965); Boahen, *UNESCO History*, 7:265–73.

44. Quoted by M. B. Akpan in Boahen, *UNESCO History*, 7:270.

45. Ibid., p. 270.

46. Ibid., p. 272.

CHAPTER THREE The Operation of the Colonial System

1. See note 1 to the Preface.

2. For details, see Boahen, *UNESCO History*, vol. 7, chaps. 14–17.

3. For some gruesome details, see Chinweizu, *The West and the Rest of Us*, pp. 55–79.

4. M. Perham, "Psychology of African Nationalism," *Optima* 10 (1960): 27–36.

5. Boahen, *UNESCO History*, 7:187-88.
6. Ibid., pp. 189-199.
7. J. Iliffe, *A Modern History of Tanganyika* (Cambridge: Cambridge University Press, 1979), p. 160.
8. G. Jacob, "Sur les origines de l'insurrection du sud-est de novembre-decembre 1904," *Actes du Colloque International d'Histoire Malgache*, forthcoming.
9. A. J. Temu, "Tanzanian Societies and Colonial Invasion, 1875-1907," in Kaniki, *Tanzania under Colonial Rule.*
10. A. I. Asiwaju, "Migrations as Revolt: The Example of the Ivory Coast and Upper Volta before 1945," *Journal of African History* 17 (1976): 577-94.
11. A. Isaacman and J. Vansina, "African Initiatives and Resistance in Central Africa, 1880-1914," in Boahen, *UNESCO History*, 7:182-83.
12. Ibid., p. 183.
13. K.A.B. Jones-Quartey, *A Summary History of the Gold Coast Press, 1822-1960* (Accra: The Ghana Information Services Department, 1974), pp. 42-47.
14. J. M. Sarbah, *Fanti National Constitution*, 2d ed. (London: Frank Cass, 1968), pp. xvii-viii.
15. Adu Boahen, *Ghana: Evolution and Change* (London: Longman, 1975), pp. 57-66.
16. July, *The Origins of Modern African Thought*, pp. 392-414. For an account of Diagne's political career, see G. W. Johnson, "The Ascendancy of Blaise Diagne and the Beginning of African Policies in Senegal," *Africa* 36, no. 3 (1966): 235-53.
17. Boahen, *UNESCO History*, 7:243-46.
18. Ibid., pp. 69-73; Morsy, *North Africa, 1800-1900*, pp. 322-23.
19. B. Davidson, *Africa in Modern History* (London: Allen Lane, 1978), p. 173.
20. Sundkler, *Bantu Prophets in South Africa*, p. 38.
21. Quoted by M. J. Herskovits, *The Human Factor in Changing Africa* (New York: Knopf, 1970), p. 424.
22. T. Ranger, ed., *Aspects of Central African History* (London: Heinemann, 1968), p. 195.
23. R. Oliver and A. Atmore, *Africa since 1800* (Cambridge: Cambridge University Press, 1967, p. 157.
24. For a fascinating study of Chilembwe, see Shepperson and Price, *Independent African*
25. J. A. Langley, "Garveyism and African Nationalism" *Race* 11, no. 2 (1969): 157-72; R. L. Okwonko, "The Garvey Movement in British West Africa," *Journal of African History* 21 (1980): 105-117; A. Adu Boahen, "Garveyism in the Gold Coast," (unpublished paper, 1985).
26. Roux, *Time Longer than Rope*, pp. 141-43.
27. Boahen, *UNESCO History*, 7:691.
28. Ibid., pp. 595-601.
29. Ibid., p. 695; B. A. Ogot, *Zamani* (Nairobi: East African Publishing House, 1974), p. 263.

30. Boahen, *UNESCO History*, 7:695.
31. For a detailed treatment of the NCBWA, see J. A. Langley, *Pan-Africanism and Nationalism in West Africa, 1900–1945*, (Oxford: Clarendon Press, 1973).
32. Boahen, *Ghana: Evolution and Change*, pp. 143–6.
33. J. B. Danquah, *Self-Help and Expansion* (Accra: Gold Coast Youth Conference, 1943); Danquah, *Friendship and Empire* (London: Fabian Colonial Bureau, 1949); K. Sekyi, *The Blinkards* (London: Heinemann, 1974 [written in 1915]); N. Azikiwe, *Liberia in World Politics* (London: A. H. Stockwell, 1934); Azikiwe, *Renascent Africa* (1937; repr. London: Frank Cass, 1968).
34. Boahen, *UNESCO History*, 7:658.
35. For further details about Harry Thuku, see his autobiography, *Harry Thuku* (Nairobi: Oxford University Press, 1970); see also K. J. King, "The Nationalism of Harry Thuku," *Trans-African Journal of History* 1, no. 1 (1971): 39–59.
36. Ranger, *Aspects of Central African History*, p. 223.
37. For further information, see Roux, *Time Longer than Rope*, pp. 74–76; H. J. Simons and R. E. Simons, *Class and Colour in South Africa* (Harmondsworth: Penguin, 1969), pp. 132–36; and G. M. Gerhart, *Black Power in South Africa* (Berkeley and Los Angeles: University of California Press, 1978), pp. 21–39.
38. Sundkler, *Bantu Prophets in South Africa*, p. 76.
39. Boahen, *UNESCO History*, 7:533–37.
40. For details on the Italian occupation, see S.K.B. Asante, *Pan-African Protest: West Africa and the Italo-Ethiopian Crisis, 1939–1941* (London: Longman, 1977).
41. On this congress see E. Geiss, *The Pan-African Movement* (London: Methuen, 1974).

CHAPTER FOUR The Colonial Impact

1. This chapter is based mainly on the final chapter of Boahen, *UNESCO History*, vol. 7.
2. Gann and Duignan, *Burden of Empire*, p. 382.
3. Rodney, *How Europe Underdeveloped Africa*, p. 223.
4. A. A. Mazrui and M. Tidy, *Nationalism and New States in Africa* (London: Heinemann, 1984), p. xxii.
5. See Chapter 3, above, at n. 17.
6. Hopkins, *An Economic History of West Africa*, p. 235.
7. W. A. Lewis, *Politics in West Africa* (London: Allen and Unwin, 1965), pp. 24–25.
8. T. Garrard, *Akan Weights and the Gold Trade* (London: Longman, 1980), pp. 127–66.
9. Boahen, *UNESCO History*, 7:440, 484–85.

10. T. B. Kabwegyere, *The Politics of State Formation* (Nairobi: East African Publishing House, 1974).

11. A. A. Mazrui, *The Moving Cultural Frontier*, World Order Model Project, working paper no. 18, (New York: Institute of World Order, 1982).

12. R. Oliver and A. Atmore, *Africa since 1800*, 2d ed. (Cambridge: Cambridge University Press, 1972), p. 275; Gann and Duignan, *Colonialism in Africa*, 1:23.

13. J.F.A. Ajayi, "Colonialism: An Episode in African History," in Gann and Duignan, *Colonialism in Africa*, 1:497–509; J.F.A. Ajayi, "The Continuity of African Institutions under Colonialism," in Ranger, *Emerging Themes of African History*,; Hopkins, *An Economic History of West Africa*, pp. 167, 206, 235.

14. Mazrui and Tidy, *Nationalism and the New States in Africa*, p. xii.

15. Chinweizu, *The West and the Rest of Us*, pp. 80–187.

16. Mazrui and Tidy, *Nationalism and the New States in Africa*, p. xii.

Bibliography

Ajayi, J.F.A., and M. Crowder, eds., *History of West Africa*. Vol. 2. London: Longman, 1974.

———. "Colonialism: An Episode in African History." In Gann, and Duignan *Colonialism in Africa, 1897-1960*.

———. "The Continuity of African Institutions under Colonialism." In Ranger, *Emerging Themes of African History*.

Ajayi, J.F.A., and M. Crowder, eds. *History of West Africa*. Vol. 2. London: Longman, 1974.

Akpan, M. B., "Ethiopia and Liberia." In Boahen, *UNESCO History*, vol. 7.

Asante, S. K. B. *Pan-African Protest: West Africa and the Italo-Ethiopian Crisis, 1939-1941*. London: Longman, 1977.

Asiwaju, A. I. "Migrations as Revolt: The Example of the Ivory Coast and Upper Volta before 1945." *Journal of African History* 17 (1976): 577-94.

Ayandele, E. *The Missionary Impact on Modern Nigeria, 1842-1914: A Political and Social Analysis*. London: Longman, 1966.

Azikiwe, N. *Liberia in World Politics*. London: A. H. Stockwell, 1934.

———. *Renascent Africa*. 1937; repr. London: Frank Cass, 1968.

Barrett, D. B. *African Initiatives in Religion*. Nairobi: East African Publishing House, 1971.

Blyden, E. W. *Christianity, Islam, and the Negro Race*. New Ed. Edinburgh: Edinburgh University Press, 1967.

Boahen, A. Adu. *Britain, the Sahara, and Western Sudan*. Oxford: Clarendon Press, 1964.

———. *Ghana: Evolution and Change*. London: Longman, 1975.

———. "Towards a New Categorization and Periodization of African Responses and Reactions to Colonialism." Seminar paper, Department of History, University of Ghana, 1976.

———. "Prempeh in Exile." *Research Review* (Legon) 8, no. 3 (1977): 3-20.

———, ed. *General History of Africa*. Vol. 7. UNESCO. London: Heineman, 1985.

Casely Hayford, J. E. *Gold Coast Native Institutions*. ed. London: Frank Cass, 1970.

Chinweizu. *The West and the Rest of Us: White Predators, Black Slavers, and the African Elite.* New York: Vintage Books, 1975.

Coleman, J. C. *Nigeria: Background to Nationalism.* Berkeley and Los Angeles: University of California Press, 1958.

Crowder, M. *West Africa under Colonial Rule.* London: Hutchison, 1968.

———, ed. *West African Resistance.* London: Hutchison, 1971.

Crowe, S. E. *The Berlin-West African Conference.* 1884–1885, London: Longmans Green, 1942.

Curtin, P., S. Feierman, L. Thompson, and J. Vansina. *African History.* London: Longman, 1978.

Danquah, J. B. *Friendship and Empire.* London: Fabian Colonial Bureau, 1949.

———. *Self-Help and Expansion.* Accra: Gold Coast Youth Conference, 1943.

Davidson, B. *Africa in Modern History.* London: Allen Lane, 1978.

———. *The African Past.* London: Longman, 1964.

Dupuis, J. *Journal of a Residence in Ashantee,* New ed. London: Frank Cass, 1966.

Fieldhouse, D. K. *Colonialism, 1870–1945: An Introduction.* London: Weidenfeld and Nicolson, 1981.

Fyle, C. M. *The History of Sierra Leone.* London: Evans Brothers, 1981.

Fynn, J. K. "Ghana-Asante." In Crowder, *West African Resistance.*

Gann, L. H. and P. Duignan. *Burden of Empire.* London: Pall Mall, 1967.

———, eds. *Colonialism in Africa, 1879–1960.* Vol. 1. Cambridge: Cambridge University Press, 1969.

Garrard, T. *Akan Weights and the Gold Trade.* London: Longman, 1980.

Geiss, I. *The Pan-African Movement.* London: Methuen, 1974.

Gerhart, G. M. *Black Power in South Africa.* Berkeley and Los Angeles: University of California Press, 1978.

Gifford, P. and R. W. Louis, eds. *Britain and France in Africa.* New Haven: Yale University Press, 1971.

———, eds. *Britain and Germany in Africa,* New Haven: Yale University Press, 1967.

Greenfield, R. *Ethiopia: A New Political History.* New York: Prager, 1965.

Hargreaves, J. D. "The French Conquest of Dahomey." *History Today,* 30 (March 1980): 5–9.

———. *Prelude to the Partition of West Africa.* London: Macmillan, 1963.

Hayes, C. J. A. *A Generation of Materialism, 1871–1900.* New York: Harper and Row, 1941.

Herskovits, M. J. *The Human Factor in Changing Africa.* New York: Knopf, 1970.

Hiskett, M. *The Development of Islam in West Africa.* London: Longman, 1984.

Hobson, J. A. *Imperialism: A Study.* New ed. Ann Arbor: University of Michigan Press, 1965.

Hopkins, A. G. *An Economic History of West Africa.* London: Longman, 1973.

Horton, J. *The Diseases of Tropical Climates and Their Treatment.* London 1870.

———. *Letters on the Political Condition of the Gold Coast.* 2d ed. London: Frank Cass, 1970.

———. *The Medical Topography of the West Coast of Africa.* London, 1895.

———. *The Political Economy of British Western Africa.* London, 1865.

———. *West African Countries and Peoples.* Edinburgh: Edinburgh University Press, 1964.

Iliffe, J. *A Modern History of Tanganyika.* Cambridge: Cambridge University Press, 1979.

Ikime, O., ed. *Groundwork of Nigerian History.* Ibadan: Heineman, 1980.

Isaacman, A. *Anti-Colonial Activity in the Zambesi Valley, 1850–1921.* Berkeley and Los Angeles: University of California Press, 1976.

Jacob, G. "Sur les origines de l'insurrection du sud-est de novembre-decembre 1904." *Actes du Colloque International d'Histoire Malgache* (forthcoming).

Johnson, G. W. "The Ascendancy of Blaise Diagne and the Beginning of African policies in Senegal." *Africa* 36, no. 3 (1966): 235–53.

Jones-Quartey, K.A.B. *A Summary History of the Gold Coast Press, 1822–1960.* Accra: The Ghana Information Services Department, 1974.

July, R. W. *The Origins of Modern African Thought.* London: Faber, 1967.

Kabwegyere, T. B. *The Politics of State Formation.* Nairobi, East African Publishing House, 1974.

Kaniki, M. H. Y., ed. *Tanzania under Colonial Rule.* London: Longman, 1980.

Kanya-Fortsner, A. S. "Mali-Tukulor." In Crowder, *West African Resistance.*

Keltie, J. S. *The Partition of Africa.* London: E. Stanford, 1893.

King, K. J. "The Nationalism of Harry Thuku." *Trans-African Journal of History* 1, no. 1 (1971): 39–59.

Langley, J. A. "Garveyism and African Nationalism." *Race* 11, no. 2 (1969): 157–72.

———. *Pan-Africanism and Nationalism in West Africa, 1900–1945.* Oxford: Clarendon Press, 1973.

Lenin, V. I. *Imperialism: The Highest Stage of Capitalism.* Moscow: Progress Publishers, 1983.

Lewis, W. A. *Politics in West Africa.* London: Allen and Unwin, 1965.

Lynch, H. R. *Edward Wilmot Blyden, Pan-Negro Patriot,* London: Oxford University Press, 1967.

McIntyre, W. D. *The Imperial Frontier in the Tropics. 1865–1875.* London: Macmillan, 1967.

Marcus, H. G. *The Life and Times of Menelik II: Ethiopia, 1844–1913.* Oxford: Clarendon Press, 1975.

Marks, S. "Khoisan Resistance to the Dutch in the Seventeenth and Eighteenth Centuries." *Journal of African History* 13 (1972): 55–80.

Mazrui, A. A. *The Moving Cultural Frontier.* World Order Model Project, Working Paper no. 18. New York: Institute of World Order, 1982.

Mazrui, A. A. and M. Tidy. *Nationalism and the New States in Africa,* London: Heineman, 1984.

Morsy, M. *North Africa, 1800–1900.* London: Longman, 1984.

Obichere, B. I. *West African States and European Expansion: The Dahomey-Niger Hinterland, 1898.* New Haven: Yale University Press, 1971.

Ogot, B. A. ed. *Zamani: A Survey of East African History.* Nairobi: East African Publishing House, 1974.

Okwonko, R. L. "The Garvey Movement in British West Africa." *Journal of African History* 21 (1980): 105–17.

Oliver, R. and A. Atmore. *Africa since 1800.* 2d ed. Cambridge: Cambridge University Press, 1972.

Pallinder-Law, A. "Aborted Modernization in West Africa." *Journal of African History* 15 (1974): 65–82.

Perham, M. "Psychology of African Nationalism." *Optima* 10 (1960): 27–36.

Perham, M. and M. Bull, eds. *The Diaries of Lord Luggard.* Vol. 2. Evanston, Ill.: Northwestern University Press, 1963.

Person, Y. "Guinea-Samori." In Crowder, *West African Resistance.*

Ranger, T. O. *Aspects of Central African History.* London: Heineman, 1968.

————, ed. *Emerging Themes of African History.* Nairobi: East African Publishing House, 1968.

Robinson, R. E. and J. Gallagher. *Africa and the Victorians: The Official Mind of Imperialism.* London: Macmillan, 1961.

Rodney, W. *How Europe Underdeveloped Africa.* Dar es Salaam: Tanzania Publishing House, 1972.

Ross, D. "Dahomey." In Crowder, *West African Resistance.*

Roux, E. *Time Longer than Rope.* 2d ed. Madison: University of Wisconsin Press, 1964.

Rubenson, S. *Wuchale XVII: The Attempt to Establish a Protectorate over Ethiopia.* Addis Ababa: Haile Selassie I University, 1964.

Saint-Martin, Y. *L'empire Toucouleur et la France un demi-siecle de relations diplomatiques (1846–1893).* Dakar, 1972.

Sarbah, J. M. *Fanti National Constitution.* 2d ed. London: Frank Cass, 1968.

Schumpeter, J. *Imperialism and Social Classes.* Cleveland: World Publishing Co., 1955.

Sekyi, W. E. G. *The Blinkards.* London: Heineman, 1974.

Shepperson, G. and T. Price. *Independent African: John Chilembwe and the Origins, Setting, and Significance of the Nyasaland Native Uprising of 1915.* Edinburgh: Edinburgh University Press, 1958.

Simons, A. J. and R. E. Simons. *Class and Colour in South Africa, 1850–1950.* Harmondsworth: Penguin, 1969.

Sundkler, B. G. M. *Bantu Prophets in South Africa.* 2d ed. London: Oxford University Press, 1961.

Sutcliffe, B. and R. Owen, eds. *Studies in the Theory of Imperialism.* London: Longman, 1972.

Taylor, A. J. P. *Germany's Bid for Colonies.* London: Macmillan, 1938.

Temu, A. J. "Tanzanian Societies and Colonial Invasion, 1875–1907." In Kaniki, *Tanzania under Colonial Rule.*

Thornton, J. "The State in African Historiography: A Reassessment." *Ufahamu,* 4, no. 2 (1973): 119–20.

Thuku, H. *Harry Thuku*. Nairobi: Oxford University Press, 1970.

Touval, S. "Treaties, Borders, and the Partition of Africa." *Journal of African History* 7 (1966): 279–92.

Uzoigwe, G. N. *Britain and the Conquest of Africa: The Age of Salisbury*. Ann Arbor: University of Michigan Press, 1974.

Vatikiotis, P. J. *The Modern History of Egypt*. London: Weidenfeld and Nicolson, 1969.

Walker, E. *A History of Southern Africa*, 3d ed. London: Longman, 1957.

Weiskel, T. C. *French Colonial Rule and the Baule Peoples, 1889–1911*. Oxford: Clarendon Press, 1980.

Wilks, I. G. *Asante in the Nineteenth Century*. Cambridge: Cambridge University Press, 1975.

Willis, A. J. *An Introduction to the History of Central Africa*. London: Oxford University Press, 1964.

Wilson, H. S., ed. *Origins of West Africa Nationalism*. London: Macmillan, 1969.

Wilson, M. and L. Thompson, eds. *The Oxford History of South Africa*. Vol. 2 Oxford: Clarendon Press, 1971.

Index

Abdel-Kader, Hajali, 78
Abdullah, Muhammad Ahmad Ibn, 48
Abeokuta, 12, 14, 15, 39, 81–82. *See
  also* Nigeria
Aborigines' Rights Protection Society
  (ARPS), 68, 69–70
Abudullah, Khalifa, 48
Abushiri, 47
Adowa, battle of, 55, 56
Africa: armies of, 56–57, 98–99, 110–11;
  boundary disputes in, 96; boycotts in,
  80, 81, 84, 89, 90; bureaucracy in, 98;
  cash crops in, 5, 60, 77, 100, 101–2,
  105, 110; centralization of, 7–8, 13;
  churches in, 73, 81; commercial
  unification of, 5–7, 102; constitutional
  experimentation in, 8, 9–13; cultural
  unification of, 6–7; disease in, 13;
  distribution of wealth in, 4; economy
  of, 1, 3–4, 61, 100–101; educated elite
  in, 17–19, 20, 35, 59, 62, 63, 67–68,
  69, 72, 76–77, 81–87, 111; education
  in, 11, 14, 16–19, 69, 82, 87, 104;
  effect of worldwide depression on, 77,
  80; exports of, 3–4, 61; food production in, 102; illiteracy in, 106; industrialization of, 8, 26, 101; infrastructure of, 58, 60, 100, 101; intellectual
  revolution in, 19, 20–23; judicial
  system in, 98; litigation over land in,
  102; migrations (*mfecane*) in, 13–14,
  66–67, 78; mining in, 61, 100, 101,
110; missionaries in, 15; modernization in, 8–9, 13, 100–101; modern
  leaders in, 91, 92, 93; newspapers in,
  68, 81, 83; nineteenth-century, 1–27,
  35; political associations in, 68–69,
  81–87, 92–93; political parties in, 70,
  82, 91; population in, 13, 95; rebellions in, 64–66, 75, 78, 79; religion in,
  14–17; rural areas of, 4–5, 63, 100,
  105; Scramble for, 27–57, 91, 102;
  social changes in, 13–23; strikes in,
  72, 78, 81, 84, 89, 90; technology in,
  26, 101; trade in, 3–7, 102–3; and
  world economy, 5, 100, 110. See also
  individual countries
African National Congress (ANC), 87,
  90, 91. *See also* South Africa
Africans: change in status of, 5, 9;
  Christian, 35–36, 38; and Europeans,
  22; Muslim, 2, 21, 35–36, 46; personality of, 22, 23
Ahmadu, Sheikh, 14, 34, 40, 41, 42–44,
  57
Algeria, 8, 93, 96, 97
Ali, Muhammad, 8
al-Mukhar, Umar, 49
al-Sanusi, Sayyid Ahmad al-Sharif, 49
al-Tantawi, Sheikh Rifa an Rafe, 22
American Colonization Society, 21
Ameriyan, Sheikh, 49
ANC. *See* African National Congress
Anglo-French Treaty of 1890, 34

A. ADU BOAHEN

is professor of history at the University of Ghana. He is the author of *Topics in West African History; Britain, the Sahara, and Western Sudan, 1788–1861;* and *Ghana: Evolution and Change in the Nineteenth and Twentieth Centuries.*